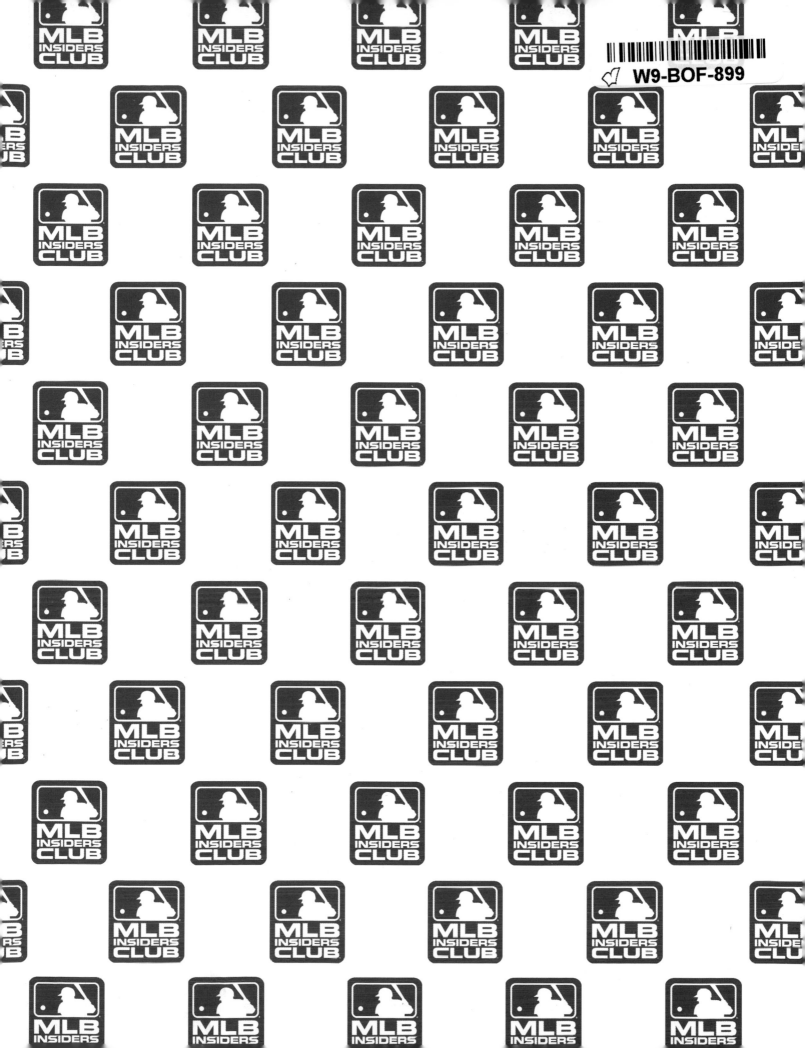

BASEBALL'S
GREATEST PENNANT RACES

Late-season comebacks, seesaw battles and the fiercest fights to the finish in Big League history.

MLB INSIDERS CLUB

Baseball Insiders Library™

BASEBALL'S
GREATEST PENNANT RACES

Late-season comebacks, seesaw battles and the fiercest fights to the finish in Big League history.

BASEBALL'S GREATEST PENNANT RACES by Eric Enders

*Late-season comebacks, seesaw battles and the fiercest fights
to the finish in Big League history.*

Printed in 2010

About the Author

Eric Enders is a freelance writer whose work has appeared in The New York Times
*and many other publications. A former historian at the National Baseball Hall of Fame
and Museum in Cooperstown, N.Y., he is the author of* Ballparks Then and Now, The Fall
Classic: The Definitive History of the World Series, *as well as* Baseball's Greatest Games,
Baseball's Greatest World Series *and* Baseball's Greatest Teams *in the* Baseball
Insiders Library™. *He lives in El Paso, Texas, where he operates Triple E Productions,
a baseball research service.*

Acknowledgements

Major League Baseball would like to thank Pat Kelly and Milo Stewart, Jr. at
the National Baseball Hall of Fame and Museum for their invaluable assistance;
as well as Bill Francis and Kristin Nieto for their diligent work in helping to prepare
the book for publication.

Major League Baseball Properties

Vice President, Publishing
Donald S. Hintze

Editorial Director
Mike McCormick

Publications Art Director
Faith M. Rittenberg

Senior Production Manager
Claire Walsh

Associate Editor
Jon Schwartz

Associate Art Director
Melanie Finnern

Senior Publishing Coordinator
Anamika Chakrabarty

Project Assistant Editors
Chris Greenberg, Jodie Jordan, Jake Schwartzstein

Editorial Intern
Allison Duffy

Major League Baseball Photos
Director
Rich Pilling

Photo Editor
Jessica Foster

MLB Insiders Club

Creative Director
Tom Carpenter

Managing Editor
Jen Weaverling

Prepress
Wendy Holdman

1 2 3 4 5 6 7 8 9 10/15 14 13 12 11 10

ISBN: 978-1-58159-455-3

MLB Insiders Club
12301 Whitewater Drive
Minnetonka, MN 55343

TABLE OF CONTENTS

INTRO

In the summer of 1916, Zack Wheat, the famed Brooklyn Dodgers slugger, suddenly found himself unable to sleep at night. But it wasn't street noise or a crying infant that caused Wheat's insomnia. It was the excitement of leading a pennant chase for the first time in his eight Major League seasons. "I was thinking and dreaming and eating pennants," he later recalled. "I used to get up in the middle of the night and smoke a cigar so that I could calm down a little and get some sleep." Such is life in the middle of a pennant race — that fundamental cornerstone of a baseball season.

Professional baseball's first down-to-the-wire pennant race took place in 1871, when the Philadelphia Athletics, Chicago White Stockings and Boston Red Stockings all finished within two games of each other in the fledgling National Association. (The A's, at 21-7, ultimately captured the pennant.) Fans loved the drama, and the Major League pennant race became an indispensable part of American life. "If there's no game, there's no pennant race," Pulitzer Prize–winning novelist William Saroyan wrote in 1956, "and for all any of us know there might soon be no nation at all."

Some Big League players wait a lifetime to play for the flag, only to fall painfully short season after season. For instance, Luke Appling, the White Sox's Hall of Fame shortstop, batted .310 over a 20-year career but never came close to participating in a pennant

race. On the other hand, there's Sig Jakucki, who managed to win just 25 games in a brief three-year career, but etched his name into the history books as a rookie by pitching St. Louis to the pennant on the final day of the 1944 season. From the infamous Merkle Incident of 1908 to Matt Holliday sliding chin-first into home plate to win 2007's one-game playoff for Colorado — every generation has its late-season moment that will be remembered forever. More than that, pennant races are personal markers in the life of a fan.

Ever since 1903, triumph in a Major League pennant race has come with a berth in the World Series. And while the Fall Classic is the marquee event of the baseball calendar, there is no doubt that the battle to reach that stage is where the most blood, sweat and tears are shed each season. Make no mistake, the victory champagne never tastes sweeter than when a team captures its league's pennant after another grueling campaign, complete with myriad joys, surprises and terrors. Players and fans alike remember where they were, and what they were doing, during the most uplifting moments of their team's pennant races. "I have never known a greater moment of pure joy in my life," Stephen Jay Gould wrote of the Bobby Thomson homer that ended the 1951 race. In this book you'll find a recap of these legendary pennant races and many others — more than a century's worth of pure joy.

CHAPTER 1

RIVALRIES

1978 AL EAST

On July 24, 1978 — the day Manager Billy Martin resigned — the Yankees were the AL East's fourth-place team, 10.5 games behind the Red Sox, who were running away with the division at 63-33. Under their calm new skipper, Bob Lemon, a Hall of Fame pitcher in his day, the Bombers reeled off a 34-13 streak that enabled them to catch Boston in September. "We haven't won the pennant yet and the players know it," Lemon said after the Yanks pulled even with the Sox on Sept. 10. "But if we can just keep playing the way we are, we can win it."

After a six-game winning streak during the final week, New York led the division by a game, but lost its last scheduled contest. The Red Sox took advantage by winning their final regular-season game — their eighth victory in a row — on a two-hit shutout by age-less wonder Luis Tiant.

With the teams deadlocked after game 162, the division title would be decided in a one-game playoff at Fenway Park. The Yankees came away victorious, but it seemed a shame that only one of these red-hot AL East clubs could advance to the ALCS. Even Reggie Jackson was magnanimous enough to offer praise of the defeated Red Sox. "I honestly don't know who the best team is," Mr. October said. "Either of these teams would be representative."

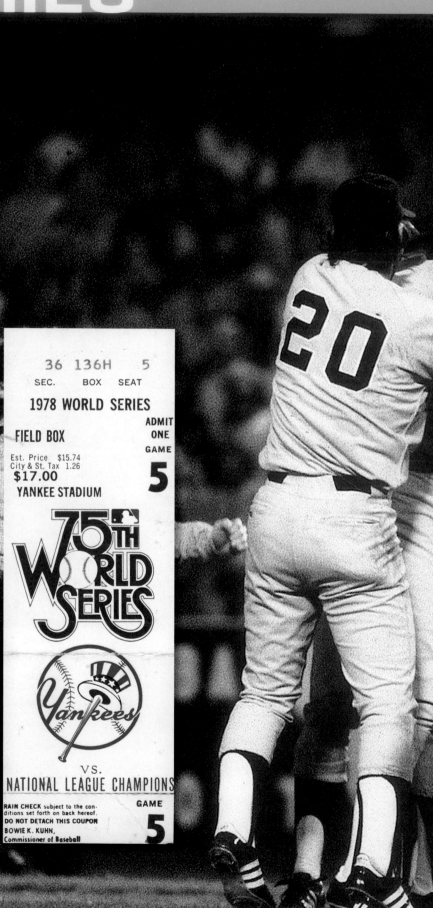

1978 New York Yankees

Martin (right)

THE BRONX ZOO

Something seemed amiss when the Yankees began 1978 quietly. But the soap opera that inspired people to nickname the club "the Bronx Zoo" merely took longer than usual to get started. After a walk-off loss on May 14 in Kansas City, skipper Billy Martin suspended lead-off man Mickey Rivers for not hustling and vowed to get rid of lefty Ken Holtzman. This led to a shouting match between Martin and captain Thurman Munson. To make matters worse, the manager delivered the news of Rivers' suspension through the media. "I'm a person. I've got feelings too," Rivers said. "One bad play I made got him mad. If he wants to get rid of me, I wish he would tell me why."

Two months later, Martin suspended slugger Reggie Jackson for "insubordination" — bunting when given the signal to swing

away. Ten days into the suspension, Martin seemed willing to keep losing to teach Jackson a lesson. "I'm saying shut up, Reggie Jackson," Martin fumed. "We don't need none of your stuff. … If he doesn't shut his mouth, he won't play, and I don't care what George [Steinbrenner] says. He can replace me right now if he doesn't like it."

The Yankees were able to do exactly that, replacing Martin with the mild-mannered Bob Lemon on July 24. Of Steinbrenner and Jackson, Martin said: "The two of them deserve each other. One's a born liar, the other's convicted." Stunningly, just six days after making that comment, Steinbrenner rehired Martin as manager, to take effect after Lemon's planned retirement in 1979.

THE MASSACRE

Trailing the Red Sox by four games on the morning of Sept. 7, the Yankees knew they would need to dominate the upcoming four-game series at Fenway Park in order to get back into the race. Although Reggie Jackson and company never lacked for confidence, not in their wildest dreams did they imagine the extent of the pounding that they would inflict upon their rivals.

In what the press immediately dubbed "The Boston Massacre," the Bronx Bombers won all four contests by scores of 15-3, 13-2, 7-0 and 7-4, respectively, reaching base an average of 24 times per game against the beleaguered Boston pitchers. The Yanks were now tied for first. "I would have to admit that they have the advantage now," Sox shortstop Rick Burleson said. "We have to pick ourselves up and give our butts a kick or else it will all be a big shame."

Jackson (scoring)

UNSPEAKABLE NAME

After one of the most tumultuous races ever, it seemed fitting that the Yankees and Red Sox ended the season tied, forcing them to meet in Major League Baseball's second-ever one-game playoff. Anticipating this eventuality, the Yanks had their ace, 24-game winner Ron Guidry, ready to pitch game 163. The Red Sox, however, took a quick lead on a Carl Yastrzemski second-inning homer in front of the home fans at Fenway Park.

After his seven RBI in September's four-game "Boston Massacre," the Red Sox had seen enough of Bucky Dent for one year. But as he would prove by his go-ahead home run, the light-hitting Yankees shortstop clearly hadn't tired of tormenting Boston. New York trailed, 2-0, in the sixth when Dent fouled a pitch off his foot, which required medical attention. He clobbered the next pitch over the Green Monster for a dramatic three-run homer to give the Yanks the lead. With 12 of his 40 RBI in 1978 coming against the Red Sox, Dent's name has been a familiar curse in New England ever since. "I told him he was overdue and that he would snap out of it," Owner George Steinbrenner said of Dent, who entered the game in a 7-for-54 slump. "It couldn't happen to a finer young man."

Dent (scoring)

ONE-GAME PLAYOFFS	
DATE	MATCHUP
10/4/1948	Indians 8, Red Sox 3
10/2/1978	Yankees 5, Red Sox 4
10/6/1980	Astros 7, Dodgers 1
10/2/1995	Mariners 9, Angels 1
9/28/1998	Cubs 5, Giants 3
10/4/1999	Mets 5, Reds 0
10/1/2007	Rockies 9, Padres 8
9/30/2008	White Sox 1, Twins 0
10/6/2009	Twins 6, Tigers 5

The Red Sox entered the bottom of the ninth trailing, 5-4. Things looked hopeful when they put two runners on with one out and big hitters Jim Rice and Yastrzemski due up. But Yankees fireballer Goose Gossage buckled down, inducing Rice to fly out and Yastrzemski to pop up, clinching the AL East title for New York. "I made up my mind: If I was going to get beat, I would get beat with my best pitch, the fastball," Gossage said. "And that was what he hit for the final out."

Rice

RICE VS. GUIDRY

When the results of the AL MVP balloting were revealed in November 1978, many fans were bewildered that Boston's Jim Rice had nosed out Yankees ace Ron Guidry for the honor. With 25 wins for pennant-winning New York and a sterling 1.74 ERA, "Louisiana Lightning" had seemed to many to be a shoo-in for the honor.

"I sent the ballot in before the season ended," admitted Lou Chapman of the *Milwaukee Sentinel*, "but I had made up my mind to go with Rice because he's an everyday ballplayer." With the Cy Young Award — which Guidry won in '78 — annually bestowed upon the top hurler in each league, some writers favored position players for the MVP Award. Dave Anderson of *The New York Times*, however, noted that Guidry won the vital one-game play-off, while Rice, who had a league-leading 46 homers, flew out in the ninth with the winning run on base. "Discrimination surfaced against Ron Guidry apparently for one reason — he's a pitcher," Anderson wrote. "Had Jim Rice done something to help the Red Sox win that game, he would have deserved the award." Said Guidry, "They should put an asterisk next to it."

Guidry

1962 San Francisco Giants

1962 NL

After the Giants and Dodgers each moved from New York to California in 1958, long-time fans of the long-time intra-city rivals feared the 350 miles between the clubs' new homes might dim what had been widely acknowledged as baseball's fiercest rivalry. They shouldn't have worried. After facing off in a barnburner of a pennant race in 1959, the teams engaged in an even better one in 1962 — a race fraught with echoes of the season 11 years earlier that had ended on Bobby Thomson's famous "Shot Heard 'Round the World."

The Dodgers began the '62 campaign strongly and scarcely let up all summer, holding a four-game lead over the Giants as late as Sept. 23. In its Sept. 28 issue, *Life* noted that "only catastrophe could keep them out of the World Series." But by the time the magazine rolled off the presses, that catastrophe was already underway.

"We lost so many close games in the latter part of that season," Dodgers outfielder Tommy Davis recalled. "The pitching was there, but the hitters didn't do the job." Indeed, after scoring 5.3 runs per game into September, Los Angeles hitters batted .234 and scored just 3.2 runs per game over their final 13 scheduled games. They went 3-10 during that stretch, allowing their rival to the north to catch them and force a three-game playoff for the pennant. After such a promising start, the Dodgers' worst nightmare had come true: 1951 had repeated itself.

Wills

Mays

FAST FORWARD

In 1962, Major League Baseball was finally beginning to emerge from the slowest era in the game's storied history. After players posted league-leading totals as low as 15 stolen bases throughout the 1950s, youthful speedster Luis Aparicio finally cracked the 50-steal barrier just before the 1960s began. In 1962, though, Dodgers shortstop Maury Wills blew those relatively pedestrian numbers out of the water, shattering Ty Cobb's modern record with 104 steals on his way to the NL MVP Award.

At brand-new Dodger Stadium, "whenever Wills gets on base a Niagara-like roar fills the Ravine with the chant, 'Go … go … go …'" *Life* noted. "I would get on and steal second," Wills said. "They'd get me over to third somehow, and then I'd score on a sacrifice fly or a groundout, and Don Drysdale and Sandy Koufax would strike the other team out."

SAY 'HEY' TO THE WORLD SERIES

Maury Wills may have been voted MVP in 1962, but there was little doubt that the National League's finest all-around player was Giants outfielder Willie Mays, who led the circuit with 49 homers while also posting 141 RBI, 130 runs and stealing bases at a remarkable 90 percent clip.

On Sept. 12, Mays collapsed in the dugout in Cincinnati and was taken off the field, unconscious, and rushed to a hospital. Doctors couldn't determine what was wrong, and Manager Alvin Dark was perturbed that Mays missed three games while recovering. (It didn't help that the Giants lost all three, seeing their deficit balloon from 1.5 games to 4.) But Mays hit an eighth-inning, game-tying homer in his first game back, and proceeded to carry the Giants to the pennant by batting .373 and slugging .712 the remainder of the season.

MAYS' BAT

A NEW AGE

As the United States was struggling to find a way to welcome racial minorities as equal partners in society in the early 1960s, so, too, was Major League Baseball. The Giants had been at the forefront, signing both African-American and Latino players, but skipper Alvin Dark had a hard time finding his way in the turbulent times. Fearful that players from different backgrounds wouldn't mingle, he changed everyone's locker assignments to force more interaction, a move he later said "went over like a lead balloon."

Initially the Spanish banter in the locker room made him uncomfortable because he feared that the Latino players were making fun of their teammates, and perhaps Dark himself, in the unfamiliar language. Players arrived at Spring Training in 1962 to find a sign over the clubhouse door reading SPEAK ENGLISH, YOU'RE IN AMERICA. It was another attempt by Dark to foster team interaction that missed its mark. Many of the Giants' best players — Juan Marichal, Orlando Cepeda, Felipe Alou — were Latin American, and they bristled at his mandate. Cepeda called it "an insult to our language." Alou played peacemaker, explaining to Dark the difficulties of communicating in a foreign tongue. "We had 11 Latin guys, almost half the squad, and it was obvious we weren't going to do it," Alou said. "We continued to speak Spanish. The manager saw that we wouldn't budge on that, and he didn't make a big issue out of it. Later on, he apologized." Said Dark years later, "My intentions were good, but the results were bad."

Drysdale

DODGERS' AND GIANTS' '62 STARTING LINEUPS		
POSITION	DODGERS	GIANTS
Catcher	John Roseboro*	Tom Haller
First Base	Ron Fairly	Orlando Cepeda*
Second Base	Jim Gilliam	Chuck Hiller
Third Base	Daryl Spencer	Jim Davenport*
Shortstop	Maury Wills*	Jose Pagan
Right Field	Frank Howard	Felipe Alou*
Center Field	Willie Davis	Willie Mays*
Left Field	Tommy Davis*	Harvey Kuenn

*selected to 1962 All-Star Game

don drysdale

Donald Drysdale

LOS ANGELES DODGERS
PITCHER

STAR CONSTELLATION

If it's true that a great team is more than the sum of its parts, then the '62 Dodgers have some explaining to do — for despite falling short of the pennant, they still turned in several of the greatest individual seasons in the history of the game.

"Talented and temperamental Don Drysdale has become not only a television matinee idol but also the winningest pitcher in professional baseball," *Life* magazine noted when it featured Drysdale on its cover in September. "Shortstop Maury Wills, a soft-spoken phantom … is on the verge of stealing more bases in a season than even the immortal Ty Cobb." Drysdale led the league with 25 wins, 232 strikeouts and 314.1 innings pitched and won the Cy Young in a landslide — a feat most impressive since it was awarded to just one player in the Majors back then. Wills broke Cobb's steals record, scored 130 runs and was voted NL MVP. But the Dodgers were much more than Wills and Drysdale.

Frank Howard, despite playing in cavernous Dodger Stadium, ranked in the league's top 10 with 31 homers and 119 RBI. Sandy Koufax won the ERA title. And Tommy Davis won the NL batting crown at .346 while driving in 153 runs, the most in the league in a quarter century. The finest moment of Davis' season came on June 18 in one of the emblematic games of baseball's decade. For eight-plus innings, Koufax and the Cardinals' Bob Gibson dueled, shutout frame after shutout frame. Finally in the bottom of the ninth, Davis rocketed a line drive over the wall to give the Dodgers a 1-0 walk-off victory. With moments like that, and with seasons like Davis', it's difficult to understand how the Dodgers came up short. "I still can't believe we finished second," Wills said. "But when the Giants and Dodgers play, anything can happen."

Koufax

MISSING SANDY

By July 1962, Sandy Koufax had been pitching with a strange numbness in his pitching hand for nearly four months — and was still enjoying the greatest season of his life. Thanks to drastically reducing his walks, the once-wild left-handed phenom was leading the National League with a 2.15 ERA. Coming off his first All-Star selection and his first strikeout crown in '61, the Brooklyn-born Dodger looked like no opponent could touch him. But the numb index finger of his left hand still "had a white, dead look about it … as if it had been made in wax," he later recalled. The numbness soon spread to his entire hand, and during the first inning of a July 17 game, the finger split in two. Doctors determined that Koufax had a blood clot and his finger was in danger of amputation.

The Dodgers, 62-33 when they lost their ace, struggled to a 40-30 mark the rest of the season, allowing the Giants to catch them in the standings. Koufax valiantly tried to return in September, but the finger still bothered him and he was shellacked in three late-season starts. Koufax still ended up winning the NL ERA title, but his teammates were left to wonder what might have been had he stayed healthy. "If we'd had Koufax all year, I wouldn't be sitting here today talking about finishing second," Tommy Davis said. "There's no way we would have lost."

GAMESMANSHIP

When the Dodgers arrived in San Francisco for the first game of their three-game pennant playoff against the Giants, they were in for a surprise. "It was a sunny day. It looked like a wonderful day for baseball," Maury Wills recalled. "Five or 10 minutes before the game started somebody came running in and said, 'You should see what they're doing to the infield.'"

Under orders from Manager Alvin Dark, Giants groundskeeper Matty Schwab had soaked the basepaths, hoping to negate Wills' speed. Although the umpires forced Schwab to undo his handiwork, it didn't matter, as the still-injured Sandy Koufax gave up three runs in one inning.

At Dodger Stadium for the second game, San Francisco took a 5-0 lead into the bottom of the sixth and had the pennant in its grasp. But Los Angeles roared back with a seven-run inning. The Giants retied it in the eighth, and the score was 7-7 entering the bottom of the ninth. That's when the Dodgers manufactured a walk-off run in their patented fashion, with Wills reaching base, moving to third on a bunt and coming home on a sacrifice fly. With the series tied, Los Angeles would live to fight another day.

Alston (right)

BITING THE BULLET

With the Dodgers leading, 4-2, in the final tilt of their three-game playoff against the Giants, Los Angeles Manager Walter Alston sent Ed Roebuck out for the ninth despite his already having thrown three frames of stellar relief on an oppressively hot day. "Jesus, I was tired," recalled Roebuck, who was pitching for the sixth time in seven days. "It was the most uncomfortable I've ever felt in a game."

On the bench, players pleaded for Roebuck to be pulled. Yet Alston left him in until he had allowed four runners. Alston then stuck with Stan Williams — owner of a 7.15 ERA in September — as coaches urged Alston to tap staff ace Don Drysdale or reliever Ron Perranoski. But Alston stood firm as Williams coughed up a wild pitch, a free pass and an intentional walk. Drysdale was being saved for the World Series, Alston said. But the Giants scored four times to win the pennant.

After the game, "Alston had locked himself in his little office," catcher John Roseboro remembered, "and some of the players started to yell at him, 'Come out of there, you gutless son of a gun. Tell us about your strategy, skipper.' ... He never came out while I was there." Even his harshest critics, though, had to back off after Alston led the Dodgers to the World Series the next year.

1904 AL

What has since become arguably the most bally-hooed rivalry in sports began modestly in 1904 at Hilltop Park, a creaky wooden structure in Washington Heights on Manhattan's highest point, where it sat overlooking the Hudson River. It was here that the first Yankees–Red Sox pennant race reached its stunning climax, although both teams had different names then. New York's club was dubbed the High-landers, after its home park, while Boston players were known as the Americans, after the league in which they played.

Boston, led by heavy-hitting outfielders Chick Stahl and Buck Freeman, held a slim lead most of the season. But a hot summer run brought the Highlanders back

Hilltop Park

Chesbro

HAPPY JACK

Even by the skewed standards of the Deadball Era, New York Highlanders pitcher Jack Chesbro was a workhorse in 1904. Wielding a recently learned weapon, the spitball, "Happy Jack" hurled a breathtaking 454.2 innings — a total that was 130 frames greater than his previous career high — going 41-12 with a 1.82 ERA. In the crucial season-ending series with Boston, Chesbro started three of the five games for New York. On the last day of the season, though, the Big Apple's biggest hero became its goat. During the ninth inning of a tie game, Chesbro unleashed an errant spitter that sailed over the head of his catcher, allowing a Boston runner to trot home from third with the pennant-winning run. Although Chesbro would eventually be elected to the Hall of Fame, he never quite lived down his infamous wild pitch.

into the race by mid-August. The race was on. Everything would be decided in a season-ending five-game series between the two teams. "The finish of the present season has been more exciting than any we have had for some years," *The New York Times* observed. "The interest in the contest in the American League was kept up, crescendo, to the very last."

1897 Boston Beaneaters with fans

1897 NL

Historian Bill Felber labeled the 1890s Baltimore Orioles as "Baseball's original Evil Empire." Led by brawling third baseman John McGraw, wisecracking shortstop Hughie Jennings and bat-control expert Willie Keeler, the Orioles posted a 538-276 record from 1894–99, including three pennants. They antagonized opponents with brawls, cursing and cheating. Among their tricks was hiding baseballs in the outfield grass so a phony ball could be thrown in when an opponent's hit carried too far. "Oriole baseball," Felber wrote, "corrupted the game, legitimized underhanded tactics and compromised virtue in the Machiavellian pursuit of victory."

In 1897, the Orioles faced off with the equally talented, but less devious, Boston Beaneaters in the

19th century's greatest pennant race, with Baltimore leading in the first half of the season and Boston in the second. Between Aug. 27 and Sept. 22 they were never separated by more than one game in the standings. Finally, Boston pulled away, capturing a series in Baltimore during the season's final week to win the flag by two games.

CROWD PLEASERS

The 1897 NL pennant race between the Beaneaters and Orioles created such a frenzy that the teams' final matchup of the regular season obliterated all of baseball's attendance records to that point. The paid tally on Sept. 27 in Baltimore was 25,390, but "one of the entrance gates gave way under the tremendous pressure from the outside, and fully a thousand people got in before the break could be repaired," the *Washington Times* reported.

Some 3,000 more watched from surrounding rooftops, while others scaled the outfield fence or peered in through knotholes. "Such scenes were never witnessed on any ball park as those at Union Park today," the paper said. The overflow crowd made it a hitter's field day, since 15 ordinary fly balls became ground-rule doubles instead when they landed among the 7,000 roped-off fans standing in fair territory. Boston won, 19-10, to extend its lead to 1.5 games. The Beaneaters would clinch the pennant three days later.

1949 AL

In 1949, two of the greatest managers of all time faced off in an exhilarating pennant race that remained undecided until the final inning of the final game. Casey Stengel was in his first season with the Yankees and at the start of a legendary run. Although the 59-year-old had an impeccable record as a skipper in the Minors, he had never tasted success in the Bigs, finishing no better than fifth during nine seasons with the Dodgers and Braves. Red Sox manager Joe McCarthy, on the other hand, owned the most impressive resume of any manager ever, with seven world championships — all with the Yankees. The battle for the '49 pennant marked the one time these two managerial greats went toe to toe.

Stengel's Yankees started off white-hot and maintained the AL lead into late September, despite injuries to Joe DiMaggio, Yogi Berra and Johnny Mize. McCarthy's Red Sox, meanwhile, were stumbling around in fifth place as late as July 8. But powered by a potent offense, the Sox embarked on a 58-19 run that enabled them to catch the Yankees with a week remaining in the season. "Overtaken by a final batch of injuries as well as the onrushing Red Sox," *New York Times* scribe Red Smith wrote, "it looked as though the inevitable finish of a gallant fight had arrived." But it turned out the fight had only begun. Its outcome would hinge on a season-ending two-game series at Yankee Stadium.

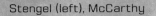
Stengel (left), McCarthy

DiMaggio (scoring)

DiMAGGIO SIGNED
BASEBALL

A JOLT FROM JOE

Although the Yankees boasted an impressive 41-24 record on June 28, 1949, they still felt a bit uneasy about their chances of reaching the Fall Classic. Four different teams were within striking distance as the end of the season approached. The first-place Yanks had spent all year playing without their superstar, Joe DiMaggio, who was sidelined by a bone spur in his foot. On June 27, DiMaggio managed to play in an exhibition game pain-free, but he was still out of shape and his swing looked rusty. When the Yankees left for a crucial four-game series at Fenway Park, "Joltin' Joe" didn't accompany them. But soon after the team left, he changed his mind and hopped on a plane to Boston. Arriving shortly before game time, he told Stengel to pencil him into the lineup.

Batting in a real game for the first time in nine months, DiMaggio shook off the rust with a single. In his second at-bat, he homered, giving the Yanks a one-run victory. "Like the DiMaggio of old, he made the enemy cringe, as he carried his team to a thrilling 5-4 victory over the red-hot Red Sox," Louis Effrat reported in *The New York Times*. The next day Joe D. was even better, crushing two homers as New York prevailed, 9-7. DiMaggio remained hobbled by injuries the rest of the year, but when he was able to play, he was at his best, batting .346 with a remarkable .459 on-base percentage to keep the Yankees in the thick of the race.

Williams

TEDDY BALLGAME

As if losing the pennant on the final day of the 1949 season wasn't bad enough, Boston's metronomic slugger Ted Williams also came as close as any hitter ever has to the Triple Crown without winning it. Williams awoke on the morning of Sunday, Oct. 2, leading the American League comfortably with 43 home runs, but was tied with teammate Vern Stephens with 159 RBI. He also led Detroit's George Kell by a hair in the American League batting race, .344 to .339.

Stephens went RBI-less in Boston's season-ending loss to New York, but Kell collected two hits in the Tigers' loss to Cleveland. Williams, batting in the ninth inning when a base hit would have clinched the batting crown, instead did the right thing for his team: With the Sox trailing, 5-0, he took ball four and then took his base. His unselfish play cost him the batting title — and thus the Triple Crown — .3429 to .3428.

UP THE MIDDLE

Slugging outfielder Ted Williams was undoubtedly the biggest star on the 1949 Red Sox, but the engine that drove the team was a pair of Southern Californians who resided in the middle infield. Second baseman Bobby Doerr and shortstop Vern "Junior" Stephens, in addition to being a nimble double-play combination, provided Boston with the kind of hitting usually expected of outfielders or first basemen.

The soft-spoken Doerr batted .309 with 18 homers and 109 RBI during the '49 campaign, while the nightlife-loving Stephens crushed 39 homers and drove in an astonishing 159 runs. The home run tally shattered Stephens' own Major League record for longballs by a shortstop, and his RBI total wouldn't be surpassed by a Big Leaguer at *any* position for another half century. The dynamic middle infield duo played together from 1948 through 1951.

A rally ensued, and the Sox took a 7-6 lead on a controversial squeeze play. The Yanks were in second place for the first time all year and appeared dead in the water.

Raschi (center)

BACK AND FORTH

With eight games left in the '49 season, the Red Sox trailed the Yankees by two games as the teams entered an unusual three-game series. The first two games were at Fenway Park on Saturday and Sunday, while the finale was at Yankee Stadium on Monday. Before the first game, the Yankees' rookie third-string catcher Ralph Houk took his pal Ellis Kinder — scheduled to start for Boston on Saturday — on a drinking marathon. Expecting Kinder to show up exhausted the next afternoon, Houk was shocked to find the chipper righty none the worse for wear. Kinder shut out the Yanks on six hits, his 13th win in a row.

The next day the Red Sox won again, tying the Yankees in the standings. Adding injury to insult, the game claimed Yankees catcher Charlie Silvera when a Joe DiMaggio foul ball struck him in the groin. The third game had what columnist Red Smith called "a World Series atmosphere … with World Series tension." The Red Sox fell behind, 6-3. With the Yankees leading in the eighth, Boston's Dom DiMaggio hit a liner. With two runners stealing on the pitch, it looked like a triple play, but shortstop Phil Rizzuto couldn't hang on to the ball. A rally ensued, and the Sox took a 7-6 lead on a controversial squeeze play. The Yanks were in second place for the first time all year and appeared dead in the water. "No longer can the Yankees win the pennant," Smith wrote. "The Red Sox have to lose it."

LAST LICKS

The Red Sox sweep of a three-game set just a week earlier left the Yankees needing to win the last two games of the season, both against Boston, to claim the pennant. Studying the Red Sox intently as they practiced before the all-important final series of the 1949 campaign, Yankees Manager Casey Stengel told his players: "I think we've got 'em. I can feel it in my bones."

It must have been hard to take such a statement seriously coming from a manager who had never finished higher than fifth

NEW YORK VS. BOSTON IN REGULAR-SEASON PENNANT-CLINCHING GAMES

DATE	RESULTS
10/10/1904	Americans 3, Highlanders 2
10/2/1949	Yankees 5, Red Sox 3
10/2/1978	Yankees 5, Red Sox 4

place, and whose reputation at the time was that of a quotable clown. But darned if Ol' Case wasn't right: The Yankees *did* have Boston's number. New York won the first game by one run, and then thoroughly dominated the second game until the ninth inning, when a Red Sox rally fizzled out a few batters too soon.

In a duel between 20-game winners, the Yankees' Vic Raschi outpitched Boston's Ellis Kinder, who allowed a first-inning run. Raschi held that 1-0 lead until the bottom of the eighth, when Kinder's replacements, Mel Parnell and Tex Hughson, coughed up four more Yankees runs. Now trailing, 5-0, Boston finally woke up in the ninth. A walk, single, triple and single made the score 5-3, but Sox catcher Birdie Tebbetts, representing the tying run, fouled out to end the season. The Yankees were going to the World Series, and the distraught Red Sox were going home. "God, the locker room was silent," Ted Williams remembered years later. "Like we were all dead."

Roberts

1950 NL

Early in the 1950 season, the Philadelphia Phillies' lead in the pennant race over the defending National League–champion Brooklyn Dodgers must have seemed like a Phillies fan's dream come true. Philadelphia hadn't finished ahead of Brooklyn in the standings since 1929, the same year hard-throwing Phils left-hander Curt Simmons was born. The last time the Phillies had seriously contended for a pennant was way back in 1916 — and even then they finished behind the Dodgers. Moreover, the 1950 Dodgers squad, at least on paper, looked like a juggernaut, with 19-game winners Don Newcombe and Preacher Roe leading the pitching staff and superstar sluggers Duke Snider, Jackie Robinson, Roy Campanella, Gil Hodges and Carl Furillo anchoring the lineup.

The Phillies were for real, too, that year, and had a secret weapon in ace pitcher Robin Roberts, who always seemed to have the Dodgers' number. When the Phillies slumped late in the season, it was Roberts who picked them up. "Brooklyn was a better team than Philadelphia, but Roberts could beat them," the Phillies' Del Ennis later told writer Danny Peary when reflecting on his team's run to the NL championship. "We couldn't win a game until Roberts beat Brooklyn to give us the pennant. We knew we were going to win that game because Roberts was out there pitching his heart out."

From left: Monk Meyer,
Roberts, Ken Heintzelman,
Bubba Church, Jim Konstanty

THE WHIZ KIDS

One of the Major Leagues' oldest franchises, the Phillies had been members of the National League for 67 years and won exactly one pennant — not to mention zero World Series titles. Even finishing in third place, as they had in 1949, was cause for celebration in Philadelphia, since it was the club's best season in 33 years. But on Opening Day 1950, when young hurler Robin Roberts beat Don Newcombe and the Dodgers, 9-1, he sent a clear message that a new era of Phillies baseball had arrived. The Phils took over first place on May 11, and Philadelphians couldn't have been more excited — pennant fever was, quite literally, a once-in-a-lifetime experience for most of them. "We realized we had a shot at the pennant early in the season," catcher Andy Seminick — who slugged 24 homers in 1950 — told writer Danny Peary. "It was apparent that our young players, the 'Whiz Kids,' had matured."

With an average age of just 26.4 years, the Whiz Kids made up the youngest team in the league, and their star players were the youngest in the group. Third baseman Willie "Puddin' Head" Jones, 24, knocked 25 home runs. Right fielder Del Ennis, 25, drove in an NL-high 126 runs while slugging at a .551 clip. Leadoff man Richie Ashburn, 23, batted .303 with a league-leading 14 triples. The 23-year-old Roberts won 20 games, while 21-year-old lefty Curt Simmons won 17. "We all worked together like buddies," Ennis recalled. "Like a big family."

Konstanty

ELDER STATESMAN

The Phillies were distinguished by their youth, but this club never would have contended without a journeyman reliever guiding the way. Jim Konstanty, a 33-year-old righty with a 48-69 career mark in the Minor Leagues, had finally stuck in the Majors in 1949 after mastering a deceptive palmball. He was the Phillies' resident oddball — "more like a professor than a baseball player," his catcher Andy Seminick recalled — and was famous for having a mortician pal serve as his own personal pitching coach.

In 1950, Konstanty was not only the Phillies' most eccentric personality, but also their best pitcher with a 16-7 record and 2.66 ERA, all in relief. He set a new league record with 22 saves and, in a landslide vote, became the first reliever ever to win the MVP Award. Without a dominant fastball — he whiffed just 56 batters in 152 innings — Konstanty relied on a steady stream of off-speed offerings to complement his famed palmball. "Jim wins because he can control the ball and knows what he's doing," Seminick told *Baseball Magazine.* "When he throws a fastball, he throws it where they can only look at it, not hit it." After his stunning 1950 season, though, Konstanty lost his mysterious magic as suddenly as he had found it, and would spend the rest of his career in mediocrity.

Robinson

CLOSER THAN THEY APPEAR

After sitting atop the NL standings for most of 1950, the Phillies suddenly became vulnerable in September. "[Curt] Simmons was drafted, Bob Miller hurt his back, Bubba Church was hit in the face by a line drive," catcher Andy Seminick recalled. "In the last week of the season, at the height of the pennant race … Monte Irvin ran into me and broke my ankle." Crippled by the rash of injuries, Philadelphia slumped through a 4-10 stretch.

At the same time, the Dodgers — who had been idling in third place, nine games back on Sept. 18 — suddenly began to play up to their potential. Jackie Robinson's .321 average and .430 OBP in September breathed life into Brooklyn, who embarked on a 13-3 run. It helped that the team played 22 of its final 24 games at cozy Ebbets Field. "The lead began to melt away," Phillies hurler Robin Roberts told historian Donald Honig. "We wound up playing our last 10 games with one regular starter — me."

As fate would have it, the final games on the schedule consisted of a two-game series between Brooklyn and Philadelphia at Ebbets Field. The Dodgers, two games behind, needed a sweep to force a playoff. They won the first game, bringing it all down to the final day of the season — a contest that would be one of the most memorable ever played in the Major Leagues.

DOWN TO THE WIRE

ALL OR NOTHING

With the 1950 campaign having come down to one last game, both the Dodgers and Phillies had their aces ready to go — Don Newcombe and Robin Roberts were each looking for a 20th win. "That was the biggest ballgame I was ever involved in," Roberts said. "It was going to be my fourth start in [nine] days, and for some mysterious reason … I had as good stuff on that day as I've ever had." In the sixth inning the Phillies took a 1-0 advantage, but Brooklyn tied it in the bottom of the frame when a seemingly ordinary fly ball by Pee Wee Reese somehow cleared the short right-field fence at Ebbets Field.

In the bottom of the ninth inning, the first two Dodgers hitters got on base, creating an obvious sacrifice situation for Manager Burt Shotton. "I walked over to our dugout and asked, 'Do you want me to bunt them over?'" Duke Snider recalled. "Shotton never hesitated. 'No,' he said, 'I want you to get a base hit and win the game.'" Snider did his best, lining a single to center. The ball was hit too hard to score the slow-footed Cal Abrams from second, but, to the shock of the home fans, third-base coach Milt Stock waved Abrams home, anyway. He was out by 15 feet.

But Abrams was just the first out, and a sac fly would still win it for Brooklyn. The Phillies weren't about to give 1949 NL MVP Jackie Robinson a chance to win it, so they intentionally walked him to load the bases. Two dangerous hitters still loomed, but Carl Furillo couldn't execute the sac fly, popping up instead. Gil Hodges *did* hit a fly ball, but it ended the inning. One frame later, Newcombe served up a three-run bomb to Philadelphia's Dick Sisler, and the pennant race was soon done. "We didn't realize how great the tension had been until the game was over," the Phils' Andy Seminick recalled. "We were drained."

Phillies mob Sisler (8)

Alexander

1987 AL EAST

Trailing division-leading Toronto by 1.5 games on Aug. 12, 1987, the Detroit Tigers felt they needed high-quality pitching reinforcements to have a chance at the playoffs. So that day they dealt for veteran Doyle Alexander from the Atlanta Braves.

Without a dominant fastball, the surly righty used an assortment of arm angles and pitch speeds to post a remarkable 9-0 record with three shutouts and a 1.53 ERA in 11 starts as a Tiger. "It's a pleasure to play behind a pitcher like Doyle," shortstop Alan Trammell said, "somebody who throws the ball where he wants it." The move looked like one of the best trade deadline acquisitions in Major League history — that is, until the player who got shipped to the Braves in return, a Double-A right-handed pitcher named John Smoltz, came into his own and produced a Hall of Fame–caliber career.

On Sept. 23, Alexander tossed a two-hit shutout against the defending AL-champion Boston Red Sox. Four days later, he threw 10.2 innings, giving up one earned run in a crucial extra-inning victory at Toronto. On Oct. 2, he took the Tiger Stadium mound for the opener of a three-game, season-ending set against the Blue Jays that would determine the AL East champion. It wasn't Alexander's best game — three runs in seven innings — but it was good enough to pull Detroit into a first-place tie with two games remaining.

Trammell

WIN OR GO HOME

It was the ultimate must-win scenario. Detroit and Toronto were deadlocked atop the AL East and about to face off in game 161. Whichever team won would clinch, or at worst tie, for the division title. "Adrenaline," Tigers starter Jack Morris told the *Detroit Free Press*. "You know it's the end of the season. There's no reason to save anything. You reach back and you find a little extra."

For nine innings, Morris and the Blue Jays' Mike Flanagan dueled, each allowing two runs. Morris departed after that, but Flanagan kept on going, hurling 11 heroic innings before finally getting the hook from skipper Jimy Williams. But in the 12th frame, with Flanagan gone, the Tigers loaded the bases for AL MVP–favorite Alan Trammell, who proceeded to knock a walk-off base hit. One month later Trammell would shockingly lose the MVP vote to the Blue Jays' George Bell, but his Tigers nonetheless beat Toronto where it counted most — in the standings.

1946 NL

Remarkably, for the first 70 seasons of Major League Baseball's existence, no pennant race ever ended in a tie. A three-game playoff, the National League's original solution for solving deadlocked races, became necessary for the first time in 1946 when the Dodgers and Cardinals ended up with matching 96-58 records. That photo finish was the result of an impressive comeback by the Cardinals, who stood 7.5 games out in July before roaring back to catch the Dodgers in the middle of the same month.

The catalyst of that comeback was eventual National League Most Valuable Player and Hall of Famer Stan Musial, who led the Big Leagues with a .365 batting average, 228 hits, 20 triples and a .587

Musial

MUSIAL'S CAP

ONE-SIDED AFFAIR

Dodgers Manager Leo Durocher rolled the dice in Game 1 of the best-of-three playoff in 1946, tabbing 20-year-old sensation Ralph Branca to make the start in St. Louis. The flame-throwing youngster had all of eight career wins under his belt, but one of them had been a shutout of the Cardinals two weeks earlier. Branca, though, was upstaged by another 20-year-old rookie, Cards catcher Joe Garagiola, who collected three hits and drove in two runs in a 4-2 Cardinals victory.

After traveling to Ebbets Field for Game 2, the Cardinals made quick work of the home team, as junkballer Murry Dickson carried an 8-1 lead into the ninth inning before the Redbirds won, 8-4, to clinch the NL crown. The two teams may have ended the season tied, but baseball's first pennant playoff was a one-sided affair from the beginning.

slugging percentage. Musial seemed to do a disproportionate amount of his hitting against the Dodgers, and it was during this season that Brooklyn fans gave him his famous nickname. "Here comes The Man," they would groan whenever Musial stepped in at Ebbets Field. Sportswriters picked up on the moniker, and it stuck.

41

Hamels

2008 NL EAST

After the New York Mets suffered through one of the most painful late-season collapses ever in 2007, it was — as ex-Mets Manager Yogi Berra might have said — déjà vu all over again in 2008. With a star-laden roster that featured David Wright, Jose Reyes, Carlos Beltran, Carlos Delgado and prize free agent Johan Santana, New York appeared to be the NL East's clear favorite entering '08. And indeed, all five played like MVP candidates. But somehow, they were less than the sum of their parts.

After leading the division by as many as 7.5 games in June, the Mets began losing ground to the Phillies at an alarming rate. By mid-July the two bitter rivals were in a dead heat, and the NL East race was a free-for-all from that moment forward. As late as Sept. 10 the Mets held a 3.5-game lead, but after that date the unstoppable Phillies cruised, going 13-3 while New York stumbled to a 7-10 finish. In the end, it was the Fightin' Phils who captured not only the division title, but the world championship, as well — their first title since 1980.

Shortly after the Phillies' Fall Classic triumph over the upstart Tampa Bay Rays, newly minted World Series MVP Cole Hamels fueled the rivalry with the Mets for years to come when the lefty called them "choke artists" on a New York talk radio show. "I think we're always going to believe that," Hamels told WFAN, "until they prove us wrong."

DOWN TO THE WIRE

Coste (being mobbed by teammates)

NO RELIEF

Even before the season began, New York newspapers ran articles with headlines like "Mets Bullpen A Cause For Concern." The team's staff had ended 2007 in a slump that cost the Mets the NL East. But early in 2008 the bullpen looked better — that is, until they lost All-Star closer Billy Wagner to a season-ending elbow injury on Aug. 2. Without Wagner, the team's 'pen became a horror show of underperformances.

It seemed each reliever, all of whom were effective in the first half, went into a simultaneous slump. On Sept. 13, ahead 2-0, the Mets gave up three runs in the eighth and lost. The next night they blew a 4-2 lead in the ninth. On Sept. 21 they gave up four in the eighth, losing, 7-6, and so on. By year's end, the Mets had blown 29 saves. "If the Mets don't make the playoffs," *Baseball Prospectus'* Jay Jaffe wrote, "they can hang a good share of the blame on a [bullpen] unit that hasn't come close to holding up its end of the deal." After the Mets missed the postseason, *Sports Illustrated* named their 'pen one of its annual "Turkeys of the Year."

COSTE-LY LOSS

Thanks to the way the Mets' bullpen had been performing, even a 7-0 edge didn't seem safe in a crucial game against the Phillies on Aug. 26, 2008. Just four days earlier, Philadelphia had trailed by 2.5 games, but a win this night could have bumped them over New York into first. In the bottom of the fourth the Phils got to work chipping away at Pedro Martinez's big lead. A four-run fifth narrowed the gap, and a run in the eighth made the score 7-6 entering the bottom of the ninth.

With Philadelphia just one out away from defeat, Jayson Werth singled, and pinch-hitter Eric Bruntlett followed with a double that sent the game into extra innings. The teams then placed a combined eight men on base from the 10th through 12th innings, but nobody could score. "It had that feeling like we were going to win it every single inning," Phillies backup catcher Chris Coste told the *Philadelphia Inquirer.* "We felt like little kids with the excitement in kind of a playoff-type atmosphere, which is pretty normal when we play the Mets." It was Coste himself who would win it, singling home Shane Victorino in the 13th. The Phils were now in first place. The Mets, meanwhile, were devastated. "The sun will come up tomorrow," Manager Jerry Manuel said, although not very convincingly.

WERTH'S SPIKES

44

STATS FOR KEY METS RELIEVERS IN 2008

PLAYER	IP	W-L	SV	BSV	ERA	K	BB
Luis Ayala	18	1-2	9	2	5.50	14	2
Pedro Feliciano	53.1	3-4	2	2	4.05	50	26
Nelson Figueroa	45.1	3-3	0	1	4.57	36	26
Aaron Heilman	76	3-8	3	5	5.21	80	46
Duaner Sanchez	58.1	5-1	0	1	4.32	44	23
Scott Schoeneweis	56.2	2-6	1	4	3.34	34	23
Joe Smith	63.1	6-3	0	3	3.55	52	31
Brian Stokes	33.1	1-0	1	2	3.51	26	8
Billy Wagner	47	0-1	27	7	2.30	52	10

Murphy

1982 NL WEST

Under new Manager Joe Torre, the 1982 Braves looked like something never seen before in Atlanta: a juggernaut. Led by the hot bat of eventual NL MVP Dale Murphy, the Braves set a new Big League record by winning their first 13 games. All of a sudden the Braves became a hot ticket, even inspiring Owner Ted Turner to sideline the team mascot, Chief Noc-A-Homa, so that the space where his teepee stood could be used for additional seats. Atlanta ironically lost 16 of its next 18, prompting them to restore the teepee to its spot. By then the Dodgers had caught the Braves in the standings and it appeared as though the Giants might also overtake Atlanta.

Entering the season's final weekend, the Braves, Giants and Dodgers all had a shot to win the NL West. But Los Angeles eliminated the Giants by bludgeoning them, 4-0 and 15-2, in the first games of a weekend trio, which meant the race between the Dodgers and Braves would be decided on the season's final day. San Francisco could only play spoiler. While most fans usually attend the season's final game for one last goodbye to the summer, more than 47,450 people came to Candlestick on Oct. 3, 1982, "for a far different purpose," the *San Francisco Chronicle*'s Henry Schulman wrote. "They wanted to see that blue Los Angeles Dodger blood spilled on the turf." And they got their wish.

Morgan

JOE COOL

No matter where he played, Joe Morgan made a career, it seemed, out of tormenting the Dodgers. One of the final instances came in the last game of the 1982 season, when Los Angeles needed a win over Morgan's Giants to keep pace with the Braves.

With the game knotted up, 2-2, in the seventh inning, "Little Joe" stepped into the batter's box. "I knew I was going to get a hit," the two-time NL MVP and future Hall of Famer boasted after the game, and he did just that — rocketing a hanging slider from Terry Forster into the bleacher section for a three-run homer. Despite the outcome being inconsequential to the Giants, Morgan jubilantly thrust his fist into the air, a gesture clearly intended for his nemeses in the opposing dugout. "I still remember watching Joe between first and second base," teammate Duane Kuiper told the *San Francisco Chronicle*. "He raised his right arm as if to say, 'If we're not going to win it, you're not either.'"

1948 AL

Virtually neck and neck from April to September, the Cleveland Indians, Boston Red Sox and New York Yankees clashed for the 1948 AL pennant. From the first day of the season through the last, not once did any club lead the AL by more than 3.5 games.

Cleveland finished 74 of its 155 games played in sole possession of first place in the AL, compared to 32 for Boston and 29 for the upstart Philadelphia Athletics, who got off to a blazing start — although nobody took them seriously. (And indeed, Connie Mack's A's soon faded into mediocrity, finishing 12 games behind the Indians.) Most surprisingly, the reigning world champion Yankees failed to spend a single day in sole possession of first place for the

first time in eight seasons. Nonetheless, they entered the final weekend just one game back, with a legitimate shot at the AL title.

One advantage eventual pennant winner Cleveland had over the other teams was that it was the first AL club to employ African-American players. By signing future Hall of Famers Larry Doby and Satchel Paige — and, in later years, Luke Easter, Minnie Minoso and Al Smith — Owner Bill Veeck killed two birds with one stone. Like Branch Rickey with the NL's Dodgers, Veeck was not only righting a wrong — providing equal opportunity regardless of race — but he was setting up his Indians as contenders for years to come.

Doby

THE 'ROOKIES'

Any discussion of the 1948 AL pennant race would be incomplete without mentioning a pair of rookies whom Cleveland Owner Bill Veeck called "two of the most important — and certainly the most publicized — additions to the pennant-winning Indian team." One of them, Larry Doby, had broken the AL's color barrier in 1947, but with just 32 at-bats that year, it wasn't until 1948 that he shined. Not only did Doby successfully switch from the middle infield to center field — where legendary ex-Indians center fielder Tris Speaker instructed him — but he also batted .301 and slugged .490 in his freshman season.

Doby was quiet and unassuming, but Cleveland's other impactful rookie was decidedly not. "Satchel Paige," Veeck wrote, "could not have been more different than Larry Doby." On July 6, 1948, the Negro Leagues legend underwent what was surely the most bizarre tryout in Major League history. "As ridiculous as it was for Satchel Paige to be on trial," Veeck recalled, "that was precisely the situation." Asked to run a lap around the ballpark by 30-year-old skipper Lou Boudreau, the creaky 41-year-old declined, saying, "I pitch with my arm, not my legs." Paige then "handed me a folded-up handkerchief, told me to put it on the plate wherever I liked," Boudreau recalled. Paige threw 20 pitches, 19 of them over the handkerchief, all with tremendous movement. He was signed immediately.

The high point of Paige's season came on Aug. 20, when he shut out the White Sox, 1-0, before 78,382 people, to stretch Cleveland's lead over Boston to three games. For the year, he made seven starts and 14 relief appearances, going 6-1 with a 2.48 ERA. Some even thought he should be Rookie of the Year. "I declined the position," Paige said playfully. "I wasn't sure which year the gentlemen had in mind."

Boudreau

LEADING BY EXAMPLE

Cleveland Owner Bill Veeck never cared much for the impulsive managerial style of his young skipper, Lou Boudreau. But Boudreau was also one of the best players in baseball, and Veeck was reluctant to relieve him of his managerial duties because of how it might affect his play. "You couldn't expose him to that embarrassment," Veeck said. "It would destroy his dignity." In 1948, Veeck was rewarded with Boudreau's best season both on the field and from the bench. The player-manager batted .355 with a stunning .453 on-base percentage, scored 116 runs while driving in 106, and was a near-unanimous pick for AL MVP. As manager, meanwhile, he led the Indians to 97 wins and a world title.

NO MISTAKE

One of Bill Veeck's first moves upon taking over the Indians was moving all home games to Municipal Stadium, the largest park in baseball. Previously, only weekend and holiday games were played there, with regular games held in tiny League Park.

Many critics scoffed at Veeck's notion that he could fill up Municipal — known as the "Mistake by the Lake" due to its empty stands and the chilly winds that blew in off Lake Erie — but thanks to his clever promotions, every Major League attendance mark soon fell by the wayside. A record 82,781 fans watched the Indians sweep a doubleheader on June 20, 1948, and Cleveland's 1948 attendance total of 2.62 million also set a new Major League standard. For good measure, Cleveland fans also broke the World Series attendance mark that year when 86,288 of them packed the house for Game 5 against the Braves.

51

Williams

CHANGING OF THE GUARD

After years of dominating the American League with few serious challengers, the Yankees found themselves with their hands full in 1948, trying to fend off both Cleveland and Boston. The Yanks endured disappointing seasons from such usually reliable players as Joe Page who — after one of the finest relief pitching seasons of all time in 1947 — slumped badly. Even worse, Cleveland was powered by ex-Yankees hero Joe Gordon, who had been callously discarded after a poor season in 1946. "The bottom would have fallen out of Cleveland's pennant bid long ago if it hadn't been for Gordon," Arthur Daley wrote in *The New York Times*. "He's slashed out 32 homers and has batted in 124 runs, most of them coming at crucial moments in crucial ball games."

Still, for all their woes, the Yankees entered the season's final weekend tied for second with the Red Sox at 94-58, with Cleveland 1.5 games ahead. The Yankees' final two games were against the Sox. But things went south almost immediately when Ted Williams cracked a two-run homer in the first inning of the penultimate game. The Sox cruised to a 5-1 win, and the Yankees were officially eliminated. The next day things got even worse, as Boston won, 10-5, "using the dethroned champions of 1947 as the sacrificial offering in what could well be an epic day in Boston baseball history," as the *Times* put it. Boston's win coupled with a Cleveland loss meant the teams would meet in a one-game playoff while the Yanks would go home empty-handed.

Bearden (being carried off the field)

OPEN AND SHUT

On Oct. 1, 1948, the pennant seemed secure for the Indians, as Cleveland led Boston and the Yankees by two games each with three to play. The Indians lost two of three, however, to the fifth-place Tigers, while Boston swept the Yankees, forcing a one-game playoff.

For Indians Manager Lou Boudreau, choosing a pitcher for the playoff game was easy: rookie lefty Gene Bearden, 28. A World War II hero, Bearden was plucked from the Yankees' farm system before the 1947 season. In '48 he was a revelation, winning 20 games, leading the league with a 2.43 ERA, and finishing eighth in AL MVP voting. "Bearden was a knuckleball pitcher, the only pitch he needed when he was right," Bill Veeck wrote. "It was especially effective because it broke down very sharply, which made

it impossible to hit for any distance." The Indians rode Bearden down the stretch, starting him four times in the final eight games. He started the all-important playoff game on one day of rest.

Boston controversially chose to start 36-year-old Denny Galehouse, an 8-8 pitcher who, as it turned out, would be making his final career start. Despite the hoopla before the game, Cleveland pounced on Galehouse immediately, battering him for four runs in three innings and sapping the day of any drama. Meanwhile, there was never doubt that Bearden was the right choice. He spun a complete game, defeating Boston, 8-3, and sending Cleveland to its first World Series since 1920. "I never tired," Bearden said. "I never felt weak. I wasn't nervous. I never lost my stuff."

1980 NL WEST

The Houston Astros were founded in 1962, but had never so much as sniffed a pennant until 1979, when they finished 1.5 games behind Cincinnati in the NL West. The near-miss whetted Houston's appetite for success, and during the offseason the Astros improved their team dramatically through that newfangled invention, free agency. Using a combination of hometown appeal and cold, hard cash, they managed to lure two of the greatest players in baseball history — both of whom also happened to have been born in Texas — to the Astrodome.

On Nov. 19, the Astros made strikeout king Nolan Ryan, a resident of nearby Alvin, baseball's first $1 million-per-year player when they gave him a four-year deal. The price for aging second baseman Joe Morgan — $225,000 — was more modest. The Astros had never fully appreciated Morgan's talents when they had him for the first nine years of his career, but now, at 36, they saw the two-time NL MVP as a savvy veteran who could instruct younger players in the game's finer points. With Morgan and Ryan added to an already talented roster that included Jose Cruz, Cesar Cedeno and J.R. Richard, the eventual NL-champion Astros stormed into first place on April 30 and held it for much of the season — until the Dodgers started nipping at their heels.

RYAN'S CAP

Ryan

FALLEN STAR

Only two pitchers in modern NL history, Sandy Koufax and Steve Carlton, have ever enjoyed a 300-strikeout campaign — that is, until the Astros' J.R. Richard accomplished the feat in 1978 and '79. A 6-foot-8 intimidator, James Rodney Richard glared at batters with a ferocity that made many anxious to scurry back to the dugout.

In 1980, the 30-year-old Richard was enjoying his best year, at 10-4 with a 1.90 ERA. But all summer something had been wrong: A stiffness appeared in his back, shoulder and arm. Richard told the club and was checked out by team doctors, who found nothing wrong. Whispers swirled that Richard was faking as a contract negotiation ploy. He was lambasted in the press for laziness. Some even whispered that he was on drugs — such were the stereotypes faced by an outspoken African-American player in a Southern city back then. "I do think that had it been Nolan Ryan complaining about something wrong, he would have been diagnosed earlier and checked more thoroughly than I was," Richard told the *Houston Press* in 2004.

On July 30, the Astros' medical oversight became readily apparent. During a workout, Richard wobbled and collapsed. He was rushed to the hospital, where it was determined that he had suffered a massive stroke. Richard underwent surgery to remove the blood clot that had been causing his symptoms. He survived, but he would never play in the Big Leagues again. The next issue of *Sports Illustrated* featured his portrait on the cover with an article titled "Now Everyone Believes Him," in which Astros players and officials, racked with guilt, wondered what might have been if only they had taken Richard seriously. "It took death, or nearly death, to get an apology," his wife, Carolyn, told *SI*. "They should have believed him."

Richard

J.R. RICHARD'S CAREER NUMBERS

IP	W	L	ERA	CG	SHO	K	WHIP
1,606	107	71	3.15	76	19	1,493	1.243

Valenzuela

OUT OF NOWHERE

The call-up appeared in the agate section of most newspapers' sports pages, buried in five-and-a-half-point type alongside other insignificant news. With no premonition of its eventual importance, the transaction was described in the most simple of terms: "LOS ANGELES DODGERS — Purchase contract of pitcher Fernando Valenzuela from San Antonio of the Texas League." The date was Sept. 9, 1980, and the Dodgers were hanging on to a one-game lead over the Astros in the NL West.

The pudgy left-hander would make his Major League debut six days later. Over the ensuing two weeks, with his team in the thick of a pressure-packed pennant race, the 19-year-old Mexico native wowed observers by pitching with the poise of a veteran twice his age. In 10 relief appearances spanning 17.2 innings, Valenzuela allowed just eight hits and five walks while striking out 16 and not allowing an earned run. He also had one save and two victories.

By the end of the season he had become a genuine nationwide sensation, and so vital to the Dodgers that they used him in two of their three crucial season-ending games against Houston. He hurled two scoreless innings in each contest, giving up just two hits in four frames, and the Dodgers won each by a lone run. Although it wouldn't fully blossom until the strike-shortened 1981 campaign — when Valenzuela would take home both the Rookie of the Year and Cy Young awards — the seed for a national sensation had been firmly planted. "In my book that's when Fernandomania started," said Jaime Jarrin, the Dodgers' longtime Spanish-language broadcaster. "Not in 1981, but in 1980 with that series against the Astros."

OUT OF GAS

Going into the do-or-die one-game play-off against the Dodgers, the Astros had a decidedly large advantage because Los Angeles' starting pitching options were limited. Dodgers ace Don Sutton, the NL ERA champ, had thrown twice in the previous three days, including an eight-inning start. Burt Hooton had started a day earlier and had been terrible. Lefty Jerry Reuss had tossed a complete game 48 hours prior. Bob Welch had a groin injury. The most intriguing option, 19-year-old wunderkind lefty Fernando Valenzuela, was unavailable because Manager Tommy Lasorda had been unable to resist using him twice in relief during the vital season-ending series. In the end, Lasorda had little choice but to hand the ball to Dave Goltz, a big-ticket free agent who had been such a bust that he was removed from the rotation in July.

Predictably, the Astros shelled Goltz, getting eight hits and four runs off him in three innings, including a two-run homer in the third from Art Howe. After Houston added three runs in the fourth to make it 7-0, the Dodgers held the Astros' offense at bay the rest of the game, but it was too late. Houston knuckleball whiz Joe Niekro twirled a complete-game masterpiece, giving up just one unearned run. "He was the guy we wanted on the mound when it was all on the line," Astros catcher Alan Ashby recalled. Meanwhile, after the euphoria of their dramatic final weekend, the Dodgers fizzled. "We begged Tommy to start Fernando," outfielder Dusty Baker recalled years later, "but he went with Goltz."

BACK FROM THE DEAD

With three games left in the 1980 season, it appeared the Dodgers had blown it. Having lost eight of their last 13, they were now three games behind Houston. Los Angeles still controlled its own destiny, though, since those last three games were against the Astros; a one-game playoff was still possible.

Don Sutton, the franchise's all-time wins leader, pitched well in the first game, but left trailing, 2-1. In the bottom of the ninth, the Dodgers rallied. Ron Cey singled to tie it while Fernando Valenzuela came out of the 'pen to hold down the fort, whiffing three in two scoreless innings. In the bottom of the 10th a Joe Ferguson homer propelled Los Angeles to victory.

The next day, Dodgers lefty Jerry Reuss outdueled Nolan Ryan, 2-1. In game three, it appeared that Los Angeles ran out of steam, with Houston holding a 3-2 lead through seven innings. In the bottom of the eighth, however, the Dodgers got a gift when Astros third baseman Enos Cabell booted a leadoff grounder. The next batter, Cey, came through once again when he homered to give the Dodgers a 4-3 advantage.

Of course, Los Angeles still had to stave off Houston in the ninth. With the tying and winning runs on base, Sutton entered for his first relief appearance since late the previous season. He induced a groundout, and the Dodgers had their third straight victory. The playoff, so unlikely three days earlier, became a reality.

Niekro

1993 NL WEST

One of the best pennant races of all time almost didn't happen. In 1993, San Francisco got off to such a hot start that it looked like the club would run away with the NL West. When Atlanta GM John Schuerholz pushed all his chips in by trading for slugger Fred McGriff on July 18, his team was nine back in the standings. Many thought Schuerholz's gamble was foolish — even Giants Manager Dusty Baker said the Braves got McGriff too late. But the Giants soon began a stretch in which they lost 15 of 21, letting red-hot Atlanta turn a nine-game deficit into a one-game lead in one month. "I've never seen such a string of things go wrong," the Giants' Scott Sanderson said.

The Giants' collapse — if that word can be used to describe a 103-win team — was completed when they lost on the season's final day. Only two teams — the 1942 Dodgers and 1909 Cubs — had ever won more games than the Giants' 103 and failed to reach the postseason. Ironically, with plans for a three-tiered playoff format to be introduced in 1994, the best second-place team in each league would henceforth be guaranteed a postseason berth. The 1993 chase was thus lionized by many as baseball's last old-fashioned pennant race. But far from consoling the disappointed Giants players, that only made them curse their timing. "Our team," first baseman Todd Benzinger said, "is a good argument for the new playoff format."

BONDS AND BAKER

When the Giants started their search for a manager for the 1993 season, it didn't take them a long time to realize that the perfect candidate was sitting right in front of them — their energetic, high-fiving, wristband-wearing, toothpick-chomping hitting coach. "He had a great rapport with our players," second baseman Robby Thompson said of Dusty Baker. "Dusty had a way of connecting with each and every guy, which is tough with a 25-man roster."

With an inspirational manager on board, San Francisco now needed a heavy hitter — and the Giants found one in free agent Barry Bonds, the 28-year-old two-time NL MVP whose father had been a Giants All-Star. With Baker leading the way and Bonds enjoying the finest season of his career to that point, the Giants started 1993 on fire, racing out to a 10-game lead over Atlanta.

Bonds

RELEASE THE DOGS

Perhaps it was an omen that just before Fred McGriff played his first game as a Brave on July 20, 1993, a fire broke out in the press box at Atlanta-Fulton County Stadium. "I know I'm the most likely suspect," quipped first baseman Sid Bream, the player whom McGriff had been acquired to replace, "but I swear I didn't do it."

McGriff, who led the NL the previous year with 35 home runs, burned opposing pitchers in the second half, batting .422 with seven homers and 12 RBI in his first dozen games. Of course, he wasn't Atlanta's only new addition that year — former Cub and reigning NL Cy Young Award winner Greg Maddux had signed in the offseason. Maddux, too, seemed energized by the acquisition of McGriff, posting a 1.46 ERA over the season's final two months. Mad Dog (Maddux) and the Crime Dog (McGriff) were truly Braves fans' best friends.

Maddux

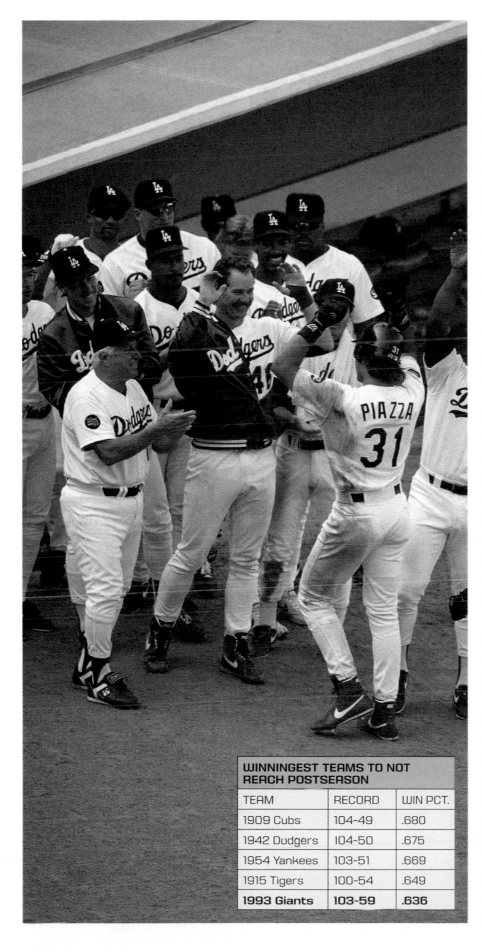

NO-WIN SITUATION

The most disappointing season of Dusty Baker's 19-year playing career was 1980, when his Dodgers mounted a late-season comeback only to lose a one-game playoff to the Astros. In Baker's view, they lost because they started struggling veteran Dave Goltz in the playoff instead of an untested but promising rookie named Fernando Valenzuela. The bitter defeat taught Baker a lesson that he would use as a manager. "That made my mind up right there," he told ESPN.com's Robert Weintraub. "Stick with the talent, regardless of experience."

On the final day of the 1993 season, with the Giants trailing the Braves by half a game, it was now Baker who had to choose a pitcher for a must-win finale. Recalling 1980, he bypassed mediocre veterans Scott Sanderson and Jim DeShaies in favor of Salomon Torres, a hard-throwing 21-year-old. Bringing things full circle, the manager trying to beat Torres that day was the same man who didn't start Fernando back in 1980: Tommy Lasorda. "We're going to throw everything we have at them," vowed Lasorda, who would enjoy nothing more than knocking the Dodgers' archrivals out of the pennant race.

To calm Torres' nerves, Baker took him to dinner the night before the game. "We had some Latin food, and prayed on it," Baker said. But prayers were not enough. The Dodgers mauled Torres for five hits and five walks in 3.1 innings, and continued the onslaught against six relievers. Standing tallest was Mike Piazza, who capped his historic rookie season with two homers and four RBI. By the time the dust settled, the Giants had lost, 12-1, and their 103-win season had ended in heartbreak. Torres, his confidence shattered, refused to discuss the game. "It hurt him really bad," teammate John Patterson told Weintraub in 2007. "He is just getting over it now."

WINNINGEST TEAMS TO NOT REACH POSTSEASON		
TEAM	RECORD	WIN PCT.
1909 Cubs	104-49	.680
1942 Dodgers	104-50	.675
1954 Yankees	103-51	.669
1915 Tigers	100-54	.649
1993 Giants	**103-59**	**.636**

CHAPTER 3

UNDERDOGS

1944 AL

Like track and field's 400-meter hurdles event, the 1944 AL pennant race was made more compelling by the roadblocks in each team's way. With World War II not far from anyone's mind, baseball seemed less life-or-death — but it was still an important diversion. President Franklin Roosevelt objected to canceling baseball during the war, urging that the games go on. "Everybody will work longer hours and harder than ever before," Roosevelt wrote to Commissioner Kenesaw Mountain Landis, in what became known as "The Green Light Letter." "And that means that they ought to have a chance for recreation and for taking their minds off their work even more than before."

With so many players enlisting or being drafted into the military, the Big Leagues took a turn for the bizarre. There were one-armed outfielders, one-legged pitchers, players as young as 15 and as old as 46. To conserve rubber for the war effort, baseballs were instead constructed of balata. The new balls were more dead, and the 22 homers hit by Yankee Nick Etten in 1944 marked the lowest AL-high since the Deadball Era.

Perhaps the strangest wartime occurrence of all, though, was that the lowly St. Louis Browns, after winning their first nine games of 1944, found themselves in contention for the pennant.

The Browns'
Sportsman's Park

Stephens

EVERY DOG HAS ITS DAY

Entering 1944, the Browns had never won a pennant — and after World War II they would never contend again. But in '44, the war deprived other contenders of their stars. The Red Sox lost 18-game winner Tex Hughson, Hal Wagner and Bobby Doerr to the military during the season. And, of course, Ted Williams had been gone since '42. With these losses, Boston ended its season at .500.

In Detroit, Hank Greenberg had been gone since 1941. The Yankees were missing Joe DiMaggio, Bill Dickey, Charlie Keller, Red Ruffing, Joe Gordon, Phil Rizzuto and reigning MVP Spud Chandler. New York remained in contention despite just 83 wins.

The Browns lost a few players but still had their stars: shortstop Vern Stephens and pitchers Jack Kramer and Nelson Potter. "Most

MVP AWARD WINNERS TO SERVE IN THE ARMED FORCES		
NAME	YEARS SERVED	BRANCH
Yogi Berra	1944–46	Navy
Rod Carew	1960	Marine Corps Reserves
Spud Chandler	1944–45	Army
Roberto Clemente	1958–59	Marine Corps
Joe DiMaggio	1943–45	Air Force
Hank Greenberg	1941–45	Air Force
Dick Groat	1953–54	Army
Elston Howard	1951–52	Army
Willie Mays	1952–53	Army
Don Newcombe	1952–53	Army
Phil Rizzuto	1943–45	Navy
Jackie Robinson	1942–44	Army
Al Rosen	1943–45	Navy
Ted Williams	1942–46, 1952–53	Marine Corps

of the men left behind to play were physical culls and athletes of extraordinary youth or old age," wrote William Mead in his book *Even the Browns*. "This state of affairs made a contender of the Browns. Nothing short of a world war could have done so."

Kramer (left)

TWO OUT OF THREE

On the morning of Sept. 29, 1944, with four games left in the season, a trio of teams woke up with a chance to win the AL pennant. The Tigers were in first place, the Browns were one game behind, and the third-place Yankees — winners of seven of the last eight pennants — entered that final weekend in the unfamiliar position of underdog, three games back. The Yanks were eliminated that day when Browns ace Jack Kramer beat them, 4-1, in the first game of a doubleheader. St. Louis won its next two games against New York, too, while the Tigers won two out of three against Washington. Bottom line: When the dust cleared, the Tigers and Browns entered the last day in a flat-footed tie. Everything would be decided on Sunday, Oct. 1.

> When the dust cleared, the Tigers and Browns entered the last day in a flat-footed tie. Everything would be decided on Sunday, Oct. 1.

BROKEN PROMISE

Sig Jakucki, the 13-game winner and 35-year-old rookie right-hander who was assigned the task of pitching the Browns' final game of the 1944 season with the AL pennant on the line, was looking for a way to calm his nerves the night before the most important start of his career. Coach Zack Taylor prohibited him from drinking any alcoholic beverages the night before, so everyone was surprised when Jakucki showed up to the stadium with a little bit of a wobble in his step. "I told him I wouldn't take a drink last night," Jakucki said, "but I didn't promise him I wouldn't take one this morning."

In the fifth inning of their game, the Browns got a welcome bit of news when they were informed that the Tigers had lost, which meant the pennant was theirs if they could finish off the Yankees. Tied, 2-2, at the time, St. Louis soon put three runs on the board, and Jakucki — who would finish his brief career with a 25-22 record and 3.79 ERA in just two full Major League seasons and part of a third — calmly sewed up the pennant by stymieing the Yankees the rest of the way. "It was, perhaps, the most dramatic finish any championship campaign has ever known," crowed *The New York Times*.

Jason Kubel (left),
Orlando Cabrera

2009 AL CENTRAL

Three games back on Sept. 30, 2009 — with four to play — the Twins' chances of making the playoffs, according to the *Baseball Prospectus* computers, stood at 3.9 percent. No team had ever overcome such odds — the Brooklyn Dodgers came closest, rebounding after having an 11.9 percent chance to win with four games left in 1949. "It doesn't look good, but it isn't over yet," Manager Ron Gardenhire told The Associated Press. "I'm not a math guy, but I believe that tomorrow is a must-win situation."

If Gardenhire *had* been a math guy, he would have known that losing the next day's game against the Tigers would clinch the division for Detroit. But the Twins won, and then swept their season-ending set

with Kansas City, including a 5-4 win in a game started by eventual Cy Young Award winner Zack Greinke. The Tigers, meanwhile, dropped two of three to the White Sox, setting up a one-game playoff in Minnesota. The dramatic winner-take-all showdown would be the final regular-season game in the Metrodome's history — and one of the Twins' greatest victories.

HOME SWEET DOME

Where to begin the story of the 2009 Twins-Tigers playoff? It was a game so unbelievable, so tense, so back-and-forth, so long, that it almost defies description. Said Minnesota's short-stop Orlando Cabrera, whose inspirational antics — and two-run homer — helped lead the Twins to victory: "This is the most unbelievable game I've ever played in or seen." And this is coming from the same guy who played an integral part on the Red Sox team that had the greatest comeback in playoff history during the 2004 ALCS against the Yankees.

With the score tied, 4-4, each team stranded two runners in the ninth to send the game to extra innings. In the 10th the Tigers took a one-run lead, but the Twins, with their backs against the wall, responded with a run of their own off Tigers closer Fernando Rodney. The Tigers looked to retake the lead in the top of the 12th when a bases-loaded pitch appeared to hit Brandon Inge. Plate umpire Randy Marsh ruled it a ball, although replays showed the ball brushing his jersey. Inge ended up grounding out. In the bottom of that inning, with a runner on second, Detroit intentionally walked the red-hot Delmon Young to face light-hitting Alexi Casilla — who promptly knocked a walk-off single to end the epic contest. "It's hard for me to believe there was a loser in this game," Tigers skipper Jim Leyland said. "Both teams played their hearts out."

1959 NL

"The National League is loaded with youngsters who have played enough to establish themselves as the big stars of the future," the remarkably prescient Roy Terrell wrote in *Sports Illustrated*'s 1959 baseball preview. "The National League could have a pennant race that baseball fans will talk about for years to come." The NL had exactly that, thanks to the Braves, Dodgers and Giants, who between them featured stars Henry "Hank" Aaron, Eddie Mathews, Don Drysdale, Maury Wills, Willie Mays and Orlando Cepeda. The memorable campaign would end with just the fourth tiebreaking playoff in baseball history.

Milwaukee led the race for most of the first half, San Francisco for most of the second — and Los Angeles at the end, when it counted. The year's most controversial moment came on Sept. 15, when Milwaukee's Joe Adcock hit a fly ball that stuck at the top of the L.A. Coliseum's left-field screen. One umpire signaled a homer, but another overruled him and called it a ground-rule double. Madness ensued when, after fans shook the screen, the ball fell into the stands in fair territory. "How could a ball fall there if it wasn't out of the park?" incredulous Braves Manager Fred Haney asked. Adcock was stranded on second base, and the Dodgers won, 8-7. "If that had been a homer," the Dodgers' Johnny Klippstein said, "most likely there wouldn't have been a playoff series."

Adcock

Los Angeles
Coliseum

BEGINNER'S LUCK

One appealing aspect of the 1959 NL pennant race was that it was played between teams from three cities that were new to the Majors. Only Milwaukee, which welcomed the Braves in 1953, had experienced a pennant race before. Los Angeles and San Francisco, both in their second year as Big League cities, reacted to pennant fever like children on Christmas morning. The enthusiasm was palpable. "People were seeing Major League Baseball for the first time," Dodgers announcer Vin Scully said. "It was different, and they liked it."

In 1954, the Braves became the first NL team ever to draw 2 million fans — and they topped that figure each of the next three years. The Giants, despite playing in tiny, temporary Seals Stadium, drew 1.42 million fans in '59, more than in all but two of their seasons in New York. The success had an impact nationwide. "People in Minneapolis and Houston and Toronto," *Sports Illustrated* opined, "can rejoice in the happy thought that what has happened to Los Angeles and San Francisco can one day happen to them, too."

In Los Angeles, nobody was more responsible for MLB's popularity than Scully. Playing in a 93,000-capacity football arena ill-suited for baseball, the Dodgers set a club attendance record in 1959, but many fans found that they were sitting too far away to see anything. So they turned to the transistor radio, where Scully's soothing baritone told fans in distant seats all they needed to know. One example of Scully's omnipresence in the stands is the time he surprised umpire — and birthday boy — Frank Secory. "Let's have some fun," Scully told his audience during one game in 1960. "As soon as the inning is over I'll count to three, and on three everybody yell, 'Happy birthday, Frank Secory!'" They did, and the ump nearly jumped out of his shoes.

Drysdale

OLD AND NEW

With Jackie Robinson and Pee Wee Reese retired, Roy Campanella in a wheelchair, and Duke Snider and Gil Hodges both on the wrong side of 30, it was no surprise that the Dodgers finished seventh in 1958. The famed "Boys of Summer" were now Old Men of Autumn, and 1959 was expected to bring more of the same. Not everyone discounted the Dodgers, though. "Their defense is sound and the lineup is full of hitters," sportswriter Roy Terrell wrote in his annual baseball preview. "With that young pitching staff almost certain to improve, Los Angeles is not going to finish anywhere near seventh again."

That young staff did indeed show improvement, thanks in large part to 22-year-old right-hander Don Drysdale, who led the league in strikeouts, shutouts and — true to his fierce reputation — hit batsmen. Another boost was the acquisition of outfielder Wally Moon, the 1954 Rookie of the Year with the Cardinals whose career in St. Louis had fizzled out. In 1959 Moon became the first hitter to figure out how to use Los Angeles Coliseum's bizarre left-field dimensions — just 252 feet away, but with a 42-foot-high fence — to his advantage. "He was a left-handed hitter but he had an inside-out swing and had a knack for lifting balls into the left-field screen," teammate Johnny Klippstein recalled. Moon smacked 14 of those famous "Moon Shots" in '59, helping the Dodgers become the first team ever to win the pennant after finishing in seventh place just one year earlier.

McCovey

NOT READY FOR PRIME TIME

"The offense didn't really get a jolt," pitcher Johnny Antonelli once said of the 1959 Giants, "until we brought Willie McCovey up from Phoenix at the end of July." In his Major League debut on July 30, McCovey went 4 for 4 with two triples off the Phillies' legendary hurler Robin Roberts. That lifted the Giants into first place, a position they would hold until Sept. 19. Unfortunately for the Giants, their season then unraveled in the span of about 30 hours. Hosting the Dodgers for a pivotal three-game series, they were swept in the Saturday doubleheader and were trounced in Sunday's game, 8-2. In first place when the series began, San Francisco dropped all the way to third. "The young players," Antonelli said, "weren't ready for a full year's run at the pennant."

In his Major League debut on July 30, McCovey went 4 for 4 with two triples off the Phillies' legendary hurler Robin Roberts. That lifted the Giants into first place, a position they would hold until Sept. 19.

CALL-UPS

Branch Rickey had left the Dodgers in 1950, but even nine years later his vaunted farm system was still churning out high-quality Major Leaguers. That was the Dodgers' saving grace in 1959, when several of their established pitchers battled injuries or ineffectiveness. Minor League veteran Roger Craig, recalled on June 19, won the pennant virtually singlehandedly in late September, hurling complete-game victories in three consecutive outings, while giving up just two runs in those 27 innings. Larry Sherry, a 24-year-old rookie, was also a lifesaver after starting the year in St. Paul and ending it as World Series MVP. Sherry stabilized the bullpen with a 2.19 ERA over 94.1 innings, and then won two games with an 0.71 ERA in the Fall Classic.

Hodges (batting)

THIRD TIME'S THE CHARM

In 1959, for the third time ever, a best-of-three playoff was held to decide the NL pennant, and for the third time, the Dodgers participated. But unlike the 1946 and '51 nightmares, the Dodgers didn't blow a huge division lead. Los Angeles held sole possession of first for six days in '59, and never by more than one game.

Los Angeles started Danny McDevitt in game 1 in Milwaukee, but he failed to make it out of the second inning as the Braves took a 2-1 lead. That, however, was all Milwaukee would get. Rookie Larry Sherry shut the Braves out the rest of the way, and John Roseboro's sixth-inning homer gave the Dodgers a 3-2 victory.

Back in Los Angeles, Eddie Mathews and Hank Aaron tried to take over game 2. In the first, Aaron doubled and Mathews later

scored in a Braves' rally. In the fifth, Mathews homered and Aaron walked, chasing starter Don Drysdale. Entering the bottom of the ninth, the Braves led, 5-2, with 1957 World Series MVP Lew Burdette pitching. Everything pointed toward a third game.

The Dodgers, though, opened the ninth with four singles. The fourth made it a 5-4 game and prompted the Braves to summon 38-year-old Warren Spahn from the 'pen. Spahn gave up a sac fly before retiring the side to send the game into extras. In the 11th, both teams loaded the bases, but neither scored. Finally, in the 12th, a throwing error by Braves shortstop Felix Mantilla allowed Gil Hodges to score. The Dodgers would face the White Sox in the Fall Classic. "We go to Chicago!" Vin Scully exulted on the radio.

CHAPTER 4

THE MORE THE MERRIER

2007 NL

For the first 12 years of the Wild Card, some old-school fans bemoaned the system. Allowing a second-place team into the playoffs, they argued, killed off pennant races. But in 2007, those voices were silenced by the most dizzying pennant race in history — a complex jumble requiring 25 coin flips to cover every tiebreaker scenario.

It was a season so remarkable that when Milwaukee was eliminated from NL Central contention on the last weekend of the season, *Baseball Prospectus*' Christina Kahrl quipped, "That was the boring division race." Indeed, while the Cubs were wrapping up their division crown, some of the most remarkable late-season baseball ever played was taking place on the coasts.

In the NL West, the Padres, Diamondbacks and Dodgers were battling it out — until the Rockies, lagging in fourth place on Sept. 18, came zooming up the standings. In the NL East, the Mets looked to be on track for a second straight division crown until, starting on Sept. 14, their pitching collapsed, allowing the Phillies to overtake them on the last day of the season. Each of these NL East and West contenders was also fighting for the Wild Card spot — a tasty brand of pennant race stew only possible under the playoff system introduced in 1994. During the final days of the season, each contender had to scoreboard-watch at least four teams, creating an array of possible outcomes that seemed endless.

Phillies celebrate
clinching the NL
East in 2007

Rollins

LARGEST LEADS LOST IN SEPTEMBER			
TEAM	YEAR	GAMES AHEAD	FINAL SLUMP
Pirates	1938	7	12-16-1
Dodgers	1951	6.5	10-13
Phillies	1964	6.5	2-10
Red Sox	1978	6.5	15-15
Angels	1995	6.5	10-14
Mets	**2007**	**7**	**5-12**
Tigers	2009	7	11-16

TEAM TO BEAT

Ever since his rookie year, Phillies shortstop Jimmy Rollins had been known for a certain brashness that delighted Phillies fans but sometimes rubbed other teams the wrong way. In 2007, he issued a prediction before anyone even reported for Spring Training. "I think we are the team to beat in the NL East — finally," Rollins said in January. It was a fairly bold statement considering that the Mets had won 97 games and the NL East crown in 2006 while the Phillies hadn't made the playoffs in 14 years. The Phillies had finished second each of the past three seasons, though, and given the club's core of three perennial MVP candidates — Chase Utley, Ryan Howard and Rollins himself — maybe Rollins' confident proclamation didn't seem so outrageous after all.

After a poor start, the Phils steadily improved, moving up from fourth place to third in late May, and to second in mid-August. On Sept. 13, they were still an imposing seven games behind the front-running Mets. But just when the lead appeared insurmountable, the Mets began to collapse, and the Phils took advantage, going on a 13-4 run to end the season. On Sept. 28 the Phillies took over the NL East lead for the first time all season, and they sealed up their division title two days later against the Nationals, when 44-year-old Jamie Moyer struck out six over 5.1 frames before turning the game over to the Phillies' reliable 'pen. It was Rollins, of course, who had spearheaded the team's hot streak, batting .348 over the last 34 games to take home the 2007 NL MVP Award.

Webb

WEBB-SLINGER

On July 20, 2007, Arizona sinkerballer Brandon Webb lost to the Cubs, coughing up a sixth-inning lead. The D-backs sank into a tie for third place in the NL West, and for fourth in the Wild Card standings. "We're all pretty well frustrated," Webb said. "The guys are trying. It's just not happening." But in the seventh inning of that night's game, the Diamondbacks ace induced groundouts from three Cubs batters. It was the beginning of a scoreless streak that would lift his team back into the pennant race.

Next time out, Webb threw seven scoreless frames against Florida. Then it was seven scoreless against San Diego. Then came three straight shutouts — against the Dodgers, Nationals and a two-hitter against the Braves. Just like that, the D-backs were in first place.

And Webb, with 42 consecutive scoreless innings, was the talk of baseball. Even retired hurler Orel Hershiser was pulling for Webb to break the 19-year-old mark of 59 scoreless innings that the long-time Dodgers ace set in 1988. "He's a great pitcher," Hershiser told MLB.com. "I'm rooting for him. I hope he can do it. We'll see."

Two shutouts shy of the record, Webb took the hill on Aug. 22. Milwaukee leadoff man Gabe Gross singled, stole second and scored on a Prince Fielder single, ending the streak at 42 innings. Webb still won the game, though. "The attention that it got, every day coming in and having to deal with it …" he told The Associated Press. "For it to be over, I can kind of take a deep breath and be like, 'Good, let's just go win some ballgames.'"

Gwynn Jr.

ALL GROWN UP

In 1993, Padres reliever Trevor Hoffman made a friend he called Little T. As in Tony Gwynn Jr. — the 11-year-old progeny of his legendary teammate — who spent many summers with his dad and Uncle Trevor. "By 1997, you never saw one without the other," *ESPN The Magazine*'s Tom Friend wrote. "Little T would follow the pitcher to the warning track to shag flies, to the weight room to do curls … He would study how Trevor stretched, how Trevor set up hitters … Little T hung on every word."

Flash forward 10 years to Sept. 29, 2007. Hoffman is baseball's all-time saves leader and a dominant closer for the Padres, who lead the Wild Card race by one game. With three teams hot on their heels, that night's contest in Milwaukee is crucial. In the bottom of the ninth, with two outs and the tying run on second, Hoffman is trying to preserve a one-run lead — and the batter at the plate is Little T, trying to beat his Uncle Trevor. Tony Gwynn Jr. laces a deep triple, driving in the tying run. Two innings later, Milwaukee pulls out a victory.

"Tony Gwynn Jr., for all practical purposes, knocked Tony Gwynn Sr.'s team out of the playoffs," Friend wrote. Hoffman couldn't stop crying in the clubhouse afterward. "He wasn't just crying," Padres Owner John Moores said. "He was bawling." For Little T, the biggest hit of his career was bittersweet. "Honestly," Gwynn Jr. said, "there was a part of me that felt guilty."

From left to right: Garrett Atkins, Holliday, Troy Tulowitzki, Helton

A RUN FOR THE AGES

Fans may argue over whether Babe Ruth really called his shot, whether Sandy Koufax was better than Pedro Martinez or whether Dodger Dogs are tastier than Fenway Franks. But one thing is absolutely not debatable: The Colorado Rockies' magical streak in 2007 was the most miraculous and unlikely comeback in the history of baseball. The Rockies' run, during which they overtook five — *five*! — teams in the standings in just two weeks, was so shocking, so inexplicable, that words can hardly do it justice.

"What's impressive about them is that they came back from the dead essentially three distinct times," wrote *Baseball Prospectus* numbers cruncher Nate Silver. On May 21, the Rockies were 18-27. They then reeled off seven straight wins. On Sept. 15, they were in fourth place in the NL West with a 76-72 record. They proceeded to win 11 in a row. Finally, after Colorado's last loss of the season on Sept. 28, they were two games behind with two games left. And once again the Rockies got up off the mat.

During the club's run to the World Series — in which it went 20-1, including sweeping the first two rounds of the playoffs — everyone tried to figure out what sparked the streak. "The one moment that really stands out to me is probably the comeback against Takashi Saito," said Matt Holliday, referring to Todd Helton's walk-off homer against the Dodgers' All-Star closer on Sept. 18. "If you want to say there was a signature moment, that might be it."

2007 Arizona Diamondbacks

ROLE PLAY

It must have seemed ironic to the Arizona Diamondbacks that their game at Coors Field on Sept. 28 was viewed as a matchup of David against Goliath — with the first-place D-backs playing the role of the underdog. The scorching Rockies hadn't lost a game in nearly two weeks, and appeared as if they might never lose again. The Diamondbacks, meanwhile, had dropped four of five and were clinging weakly to a one-game lead in the NL West. But Brandon Webb, as he had done all year long, rescued his club when it most needed saving. The sinkerballer held the Rockies to two runs in seven innings, handing Colorado the only loss it would suffer over a 38-day span — and thereby clinching a playoff spot for Arizona by the slimmest of margins.

Glavine (right)

UNBELIEVABLE

"Many baseball teams have lost a lead down the stretch," Tim Marchman wrote of the 2007 Mets, "but few, if any, have become the center of a temporal dislocation in which the precise same thing happens at the precise same moment, every single day." Marchman and others pinned the Mets' historic collapse on the clockwork-like blown leads by the bullpen, but in reality the starting pitchers also helped squander a seven-game lead with 17 games remaining. Mets hurlers posted an overall 6.17 ERA during the season-ending 5-12 skid, while their hitters scored an excellent 5.8 runs per game. As horrific as that pitching performance was, New York still entered the final game of the season with a shot at the playoffs — until legendary lefty Tom Glavine was rocked for seven runs in one-third of an inning by the Florida Marlins, en route to an 8-1 loss that clinched the Mets' collapse.

Holliday (center),
Hurdle (right)

HOMEWARD BOUND

It was fitting that the 2007 NL Wild Card came down to a playoff game — and that the extra-inning contest became hailed as an all-time classic. "With the game unfolding the way it did, you just go 'Wow!'" Rockies Manager Clint Hurdle told the *Denver Post*.

The Padres sent eventual NL Cy Young winner Jake Peavy to the mound at Coors Field, but the Rockies ripped him for six runs. The Padres stormed back, though, and the game went into extra innings tied, 6-6. Both teams stranded runners, before Scott Hairston appeared to save the Padres with a two-run blast in the 13th.

But it wasn't over. Kazuo Matsui and Troy Tulowitzki led off the bottom of the inning with doubles against saves king Trevor Hoffman. Matt Holliday then hit a triple to right — a hit that not only

tied the game, but also won him the NL batting and RBI crowns. After an intentional pass to Todd Helton, Jamey Carroll laced a hit to right. Holliday tagged and slid home at the exact moment Brian Giles' throw arrived, banging his chin on the ground. The ball slipped past catcher Michael Barrett, and after a brief hesitation, umpire Tim McClelland ruled the bleeding Holliday safe. Replays revealed that all three men might have failed: Barrett missed the ball, Holliday may have missed the plate and McClelland may have missed the call. "Matt Holliday still has not touched home plate," the *Denver Post*'s Mark Kiszla admitted. But the Rockies didn't care: They were playoff-bound. "I don't even know what happened on the play, to tell the truth," Holliday said. "I was laying there. I was dazed."

Red Sox celebrate
clinching the 1967
AL pennant

1967 AL

"With only six weeks left in the season, let's take a quick look at the close-packed American League standings," *Sports Illustrated*'s Mark Mulvoy wrote in 1967. "There are Minnesota and Chicago and Detroit and California and Boston ... *Boston*? That can't be the Red Sox in the pennant race, can it? Certainly these are not the same Boston Red Sox we have been laughing at all these years."

Although it may surprise the young citizens of Red Sox Nation, there was a time when Boston wasn't a juggernaut — when the Sox were a downright laughingstock. In the two decades before 1967, they had finished in seventh place twice, eighth twice, ninth twice — and first never. But with a phenomenally talented young roster — Tony Conigliaro, George Scott, Rico Petrocelli, Reggie Smith and Jim Lonborg were among their stars aged 25 or younger — the Sox managed to reach a first-place tie in August, allowing their fans to believe that the "Impossible Dream" might finally come true.

Entering the season's final weekend, the AL standings were packed tightly. The Twins led, but the Tigers, White Sox and Red Sox were also within a game and a half of first place. With each of the four teams having a legitimate shot at the pennant, fans were awaiting one of the most exciting weekends of baseball in several years. With everything at stake, baseball's perennial also-rans finally came through when it mattered most.

Yastrzemski

YAZ

Debuting in 1961 as Ted Williams' replacement, Carl Yastrzemski was outstanding from day one, yet still disappointing. "Playing all those years with a second-division club that never cared killed me," he said. According to a brutal assessment by *Sports Illustrated*, he "played like a spoiled brat during most of those years." But in 1967, after he was stripped of his role as team captain, he suddenly became the leader everyone thought he could be.

"Yaz" won the AL Triple Crown in '67 with a .326 average, 44 homers and 121 RBI, and his defense was just as eye-catching. "He's the best left fielder I've ever seen," Twins coach Billy Martin said. Having mastered the intricacies of playing in front of the Green Monster, Yaz threw out four runners at home plate in a single August homestand. But most impressive was the way he pushed the Red Sox to the pennant during the season's tense final days, carrying them as no player has carried a team before or since.

From Aug. 19 through season's end, Yastrzemski batted .323 and slugged .723, but he was even more stunning during the final two weeks. During those 15 vitally important games, Yaz batted a jaw-dropping .491 with five homers, six doubles and 18 RBI. In the final two games of the season he went 7 for 8 and drove in six runs. "People will remember him for providing the spark to a team that had entered the season as a 100-to-1 shot," *SI* wrote when naming Yaz its "Sportsman of the Year," "and leading it through the wildest pennant race Major League Baseball has ever had."

Lonborg

WHAT THE DOCTOR ORDERED

On Oct. 1, 1967, the Red Sox and Twins played what *Sports Illustrated*'s William Leggett called "the vital game of the longest, daffiest and most desperate American League pennant race in history." Minnesota and Boston were tied for first, with Detroit lurking half a game behind and the White Sox having been eliminated the day before. "In bullfighting, I understand that the moment of truth usually comes sometime around 4 in the afternoon," Twins skipper Cal Ermer said. "I have a feeling that it will come a lot earlier today." Indeed it did. Minnesota scored one run in both the first and third, but Boston lowered the boom in the sixth, scoring five times to put the game away. Jim Lonborg, a former Stanford pre-med student and the eventual AL Cy Young winner, hurled a complete game. Combined with a Detroit loss, Boston's win was enough to give the Sox the flag.

BEAN TOWN

Tony Conigliaro was "Boston's answer to Joe Namath," *Sports Illustrated* wrote. Tony C. debuted in 1964, at age 19, and played 111 games in his rookie campaign, establishing himself as a key cog in the Red Sox's lineup. The king of Boston by age 22, Conigliaro loved driving his Corvette around Beantown, enjoying the nightlife, and even recording hit songs in his spare time. He was also, of course, one of the Major Leagues' premier sluggers, having become the youngest AL player ever to hit 100 career homers. But that ended in horrifying fashion on Aug. 18, 1967, when a fastball from California's Jack Hamilton struck Conigliaro below the temple and shattered his cheekbone. He made the first of many comeback attempts the next spring, but his vision was permanently impaired. Instead of a Hall of Famer, Tony C. tragically became the ultimate story of what might have been.

The king of Boston by age 22, Conigliaro loved driving his Corvette around Beantown, enjoying the nightlife, and even recording hit songs in his spare time.

Cobb (sliding)

1908 AL

While the 1908 National League pennant race is justly recognized as one of baseball's greatest ever, many forget that the Junior Circuit that year also featured an extraordinary battle for the flag. Four teams — the Chicago White Sox, Cleveland Naps (later the Indians), Detroit Tigers and St. Louis Browns — each spent a significant portion of the season in first place.

By the time the final days of the regular season approached, St. Louis had dropped in the standings, but they still had a chance to play spoiler against Cleveland. Nap Lajoie and "the Naps" needed a sweep to stay alive, but were eliminated when the Browns beat them on the second-to-last day. That meant the final game of the season between Chicago and Detroit would be a winner-takes-all contest for the pennant. It ended up being a cakewalk for Ty Cobb's Tigers, who breezed, 7-0, behind the pitching of "Wild" Bill Donovan, capping a 25-4 campaign for the righty.

Unfortunately, the Tigers' title highlighted the unfairness of American League rules at the time. Unlike the Senior Circuit, the AL didn't yet have a rule requiring teams to reschedule postponed games that affected the pennant race. So while the Naps went 90-64, the Tigers won the pennant by going 90-63 — having one less loss thanks to a rained-out game they failed to make up.

LATE PERFECTION

In more than a century of Big League baseball, just two pitchers boast career ERAs below 2.00: Big Ed Walsh of the White Sox and Addie Joss of the Cleveland Naps. In 1908 their two clubs were among those fighting for the AL pennant, so it was fitting that the future Hall of Famers faced off in a crucial contest on Oct. 2 — and that it turned into arguably the greatest pitchers' duel of all time.

Walsh was dominant, striking out 15 while allowing just four hits, but he gave up a run on a botched pickoff attempt and a wild pitch. That one run was all Joss would need, for the Cleveland ace hurled the fourth perfect game in baseball history. "I am sorry we lost, of course," Walsh said, "but seeing that we did have to lose, I am glad that Addie took down a record that goes to so few."

Seaver

1973 NL EAST

"The zaniest race in baseball," observed *Sports Illustrated* in September 1973, "spans the entire fratricidal NL East." Indeed, the contenders in that division spent so much time beating each other up that the team left standing at the end — the New York Mets — became, with an 82-79 record, the worst pennant-winning club in baseball history.

On the morning of Sept. 23, 1973, five of the six NL East clubs stood within 2.5 games of first place. All were mediocre teams, each with significant strengths and equally glaring weaknesses. The Mets, four years removed from their 1969 miracle, were in first place at one game over .500. They had snatched the division lead just days earlier when eventual 1973 Cy Young winner Tom Seaver topped Pittsburgh.

The Pirates, powered by Willie Stargell's career year, were 75-76. The Montreal Expos, an expansion club in just its fifth season, surprised everyone by hanging in at 75-78. The Cardinals, despite having no player with more than 12 home runs, had spent most of August in first place before falling to 76-79. And, of course, there were the Cubs, in contention at 75-79 even though each member of their starting rotation boasted a losing record. With just a week left in the season, the only team without a chance was Philadelphia, despite the presence of a power-packed lineup and reigning Cy Young winner Steve Carlton.

Clemente

NO REPLACEMENT

On April 6, 1973, the Pirates played their first game in 18 years without franchise icon Roberto Clemente on the roster. "I feel bad being here," catcher Manny Sanguillen said. "I wish there was somebody in right field to talk to."

Clemente, who took over right field at Forbes Field in 1955, perished in a New Year's Eve plane crash while on a humanitarian mission to Nicaragua. The Puerto Rico–born Hall of Famer left not only an emotional hole but a baseball void, too. His right field job was split between four players, but without his potent bat in the lineup, the team batting average fell from .274 to .261. During his career, Clemente raked at a .317 clip, amassing 3,000 hits. Pittsburgh missed the playoffs by 2.5 games, and it wasn't difficult to believe that Clemente's presence could have closed that gap. "It really hurt our ballclub," outfielder Dave Cash admitted.

LOSING THE ZONE

In the early 1970s, there were few better pitchers in baseball than Steve Blass. In the 1971 World Series, the Pirates' righty pitched a complete-game four-hitter to win Game 7. He would follow that up with 19 wins and a 2.49 ERA in 1972. But everything came crashing down in 1973, when Blass — for reasons nobody has ever been able to explain — suddenly found himself unable to throw strikes. He had eight games with at least five walks, and his 8.5 free passes per nine innings was the sixth-worst mark in history. In August, with Blass' ERA standing at 10.40, the Pirates announced that their longtime ace would be benched for the pennant race. Without their Opening Day starter to pitch big games down the stretch, the Pirates succumbed in the final days of the season.

Blass tried everything from meditation to sports psychology to regain his control, but nothing worked, and he was forced to retire in 1974 after one mop-up appearance. "Instead of snapping out of it," he told *Sports Illustrated*, "I got progressively worse." Nowadays, the sudden inability to throw strikes is referred to as "Steve Blass Disease."

McGraw

Mays

DON'T STOP BELIEVING

Although he had long since established himself as one of base-ball's best relievers, the Mets' Tug McGraw was undergoing a crisis in 1973. "I didn't have any idea how to throw the base-ball," he wrote in his autobiography. "It was as though I had never played before in my entire life." In mid-July McGraw's ERA stood at a ghastly 6.17, and the Mets tried everything to shock him out of it, even moving him from the bullpen into the starting rotation.

To inspire himself out of the dol-drums, the Californian dreamt up a slogan — "Ya Gotta Believe!" — and spouted it at every opportunity. After two starts McGraw returned to the bullpen and posted a sparkling 1.65 ERA the rest of the sea-son, finishing the campaign with 25 saves. Thanks in part to McGraw's infectious cry, the Mets did, indeed, believe, and be-came NL champions.

To inspire himself out of the doldrums, the Californian dreamt up a slogan — "Ya Gotta Believe!" — and spouted it at every opportunity.

CLOSING THE DOOR

On Oct. 1, 1973, the Mets' task was simple: Win, and reach the playoffs. The many holdovers from the 1969 club were eager to get back to the promised land, and recently acquired Big Apple icon Willie Mays, playing his final season, wanted one last hurrah. New York's closest pursuers in the NL East, the Cardinals, had finished their season and stood one game behind. All the Mets had to do was win either of their last two games against the Cubs.

Cardinals Tim McCarver and Joe Torre, hoping for a one-game playoff in New York the next day, traveled to Atlantic City, N.J., and watched the Mets on television. What they saw whetted their appetite, as Tom Seaver struggled through six frames. But Tug McGraw came to New York's rescue with three frames of scoreless relief, and the Mets managed enough hitting to win, 6-4. There would be no one-game playoff after all.

1915 FEDERAL LEAGUE

Every so often during the early years of professional baseball, a new league would challenge the superiority of Major League Baseball, but these startups most often met a speedy demise. The Union Association and the Players League folded after one season each in 1884 and 1890, respectively. The United States League failed to get off the ground in 1913, as did Branch Rickey's Continental League in 1960. Only the American League, which began as an outlaw circuit in 1901, has successfully elbowed its way into the establishment.

In 1914 and '15, the Federal League became the only other outlaw league to enjoy a modicum of success. The Feds fought the AL and NL to a draw, stealing their players, moving into cities those leagues had abandoned — and, in 1915, staging the tightest pennant race in baseball history. Five of the eight FL clubs held first place after Aug. 21, and when the dust settled at season's end, the top three contenders had just half a game separating them. Alas, the Feds were plagued by the same problem that had undermined the AL race in 1908: no rule requiring that postponed games be made up. The St. Louis Terriers, with an 87-67 record, and the Chicago Whales, at 86-66, ended 1915 virtually tied. But since the Whales had failed to make up two rained-out games, they won the flag by virtue of a slightly higher winning percentage, .566 to .565.

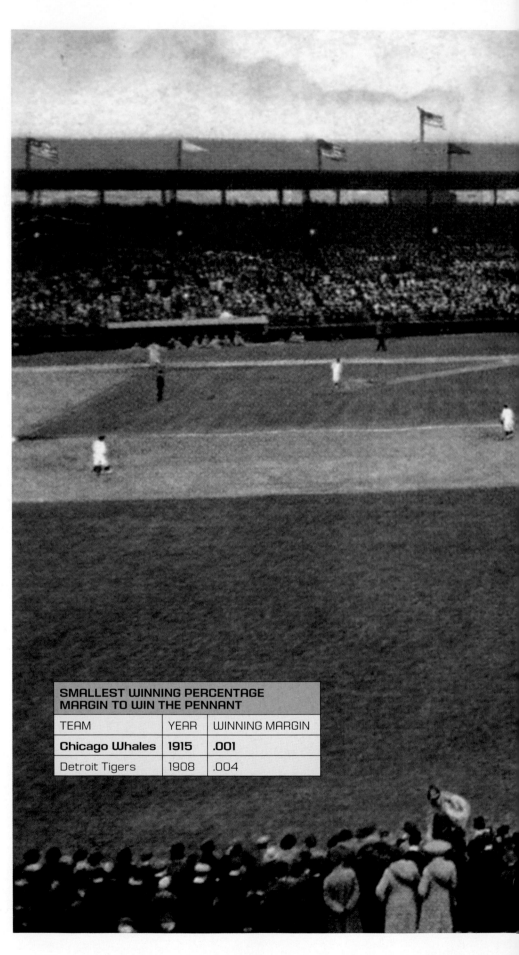

SMALLEST WINNING PERCENTAGE MARGIN TO WIN THE PENNANT		
TEAM	YEAR	WINNING MARGIN
Chicago Whales	1915	.001
Detroit Tigers	1908	.004

Postcard depicting
Federal League Ball Park

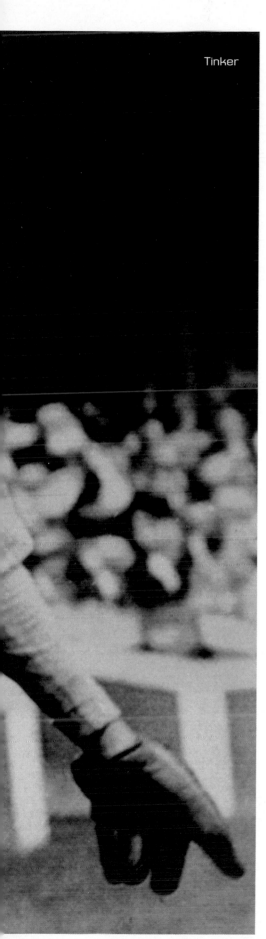

Tinker

ALL'S FAIR

When the Federal League announced its intention to vie for Major League status in August 1913, the question was where would all of its players come from? The Feds answered that query the same way the American League had back in 1901: They would steal players from the already established leagues. Of the 264 men who eventually played in the Federal League, 81 were ex-AL or ex-NL players, and 43 had broken their contracts in those leagues to sign with the Feds. Many were superstars. Joe Tinker, the legendary Cub, took a lucrative payday to jump from the Reds to the Whales. Mordecai "Three-Finger" Brown, another former Cubs hero, defected to St. Louis. Star pitchers Chief Bender and Eddie Plank abandoned Connie Mack's A's to play with Federal League clubs in Baltimore and St. Louis, respectively.

Needless to say, the older leagues were furious. The Federal League had blatantly ignored the reserve clause — the language in all MLB contracts that legally bound every player to his team for life. Scads of lawsuits were filed. The Federal League, in its defense, argued that the reserve clause was illegal to begin with, and that its language was vague. "The series of recent legal battles," *Baseball Magazine* said, "have thrown the baseball world into an upheaval, and … threaten to wreck the entire game."

Several courts issued injunctions preventing Federal League players from taking the field for their new teams. For instance, Armando Marsans, a speedy outfielder who had signed a three-year, $21,000 contract with the St. Louis Terriers, was sidelined because of a lawsuit filed by his old team, the Cincinnati Reds. While Marsans idled away his summer months shark fishing in his native Havana, Cuba, his Terriers were in a dogfight for the pennant. The injunction was thrown out and Marsans was eventually allowed to resume play on Aug. 20, but St. Louis ended the season one victory shy of the championship. Had Marsans, then a .302 career hitter, been able to play all year, things might have turned out differently.

CLARK AND ADDISON

Until 1914, Chicago boasted two popular Major League teams, but neither catered to the North Side. The White Sox played on the South Side at Comiskey Park, the Cubs on the West Side at Wolcott and Polk. Enter Charles Weeghman, the owner of the Federal League's new Chicago Whales. Weeghman purchased a plot of land at North Clark and West Addison streets, built a grand ballpark there, and named it after himself. When the Federal League went out of business after 1915, the Cubs moved into Weeghman Park and eventually renamed it Wrigley Field.

But during that final Federal League season, "the Friendly Confines" witnessed its first pennant race, and it was a doozy. To edge St. Louis for the pennant the Whales needed at least one win in a season-ending doubleheader against the Pittsburgh Rebels. If the Rebels swept, though, the flag would be theirs. Pittsburgh made things interesting when, trailing the opener, 4-1, in the ninth, they mounted a rally to tie it before winning in the 11th. Everything now came down to one winner-take-all game — and because the opener had taken so long, there was scarcely enough daylight left to play the nightcap. But southpaw Bill Bailey, pitching just his fifth game for the Whales, spun a two-hit masterpiece, and when play was halted by darkness in the middle of the seventh, Chicago had a 3-0 lead. By virtue of the conveniently shortened game, the Whales were champs, and the North Side had its first pennant to fly.

Snider

1956 NL

Even one of America's most accomplished writers seemed to strain for the proper words to describe the breathtaking 1956 NL pennant race between the Brooklyn Dodgers, Milwaukee Braves and Cincinnati Reds. "Isn't that alone almost enough to live for?" Pulitzer Prize winner William Saroyan gushed about the late-season drama. "To witness so pure a demonstration of the unaccountable way by which the human spirit achieves stunning, unbelievable grandeur?"

The Reds bowed out of the pennant chase on Sept. 29, leaving the Dodgers and Braves as the last two teams in the running. It was a race in which Brooklyn had a vital advantage: experience. The team's core stars — Jackie Robinson, Pee Wee Reese, Duke Snider, Roy Campanella, Gil Hodges, Carl Furillo and Don Newcombe — had figured in the last 10 NL pennant races, seven of which were decided by five games or fewer. The Braves, with the exception of Warren Spahn, were youngsters dealing with late-season pressure for the first time. "You looked into their dugout and you realized that if you hit any of them real easy on the head, they would have cracked," the Dodgers' Randy Jackson told author Danny Peary. "They had never been there before, fighting for a pennant, and they were just sitting on eggshells." In the end experience won out, as the Dodgers edged the Braves by one game.

UNEXPECTED HERO

There were few pitchers that Brooklyn Dodgers fans hated more than the Giants' Sal Maglie — the scowling right-hander with a perennial five o'clock shadow who always seemed to stand between the Dodgers and victory. Among other things, Maglie had been the opposing pitcher in the most infamous game in Dodgers history: the Bobby Thomson 1951 playoff. To Dodgers fans he was "a cold-blooded, hard-boiled, unsmiling gangster of a pitcher," Robert Creamer wrote. But in mid-1956, Maglie was shockingly acquired by Brooklyn. In a hugely important game on Sept. 25, with the Dodgers half a game behind first-place Milwaukee, Maglie pitched a no-hitter against Philadelphia. All of a sudden Brooklyn's nemesis was transformed into, as Creamer put it, "a villain reformed."

Dodgers players mob Maglie

Newcombe

Newcombe was enjoying his greatest season yet, at 26-7, and would win both the MVP and Cy Young awards.

BIG GAME HUNTER

In September 1956, Brooklyn pitcher Don Newcombe owned an astonishing career record of 112-48, but nonetheless had a reputation — not entirely undeserved — for caving in big games. Newcombe was enjoying his greatest season yet, at 26-7, and would win both the MVP and Cy Young awards. But there were still those who wondered if it was wise to start him in the crucial regular-season finale, with the Dodgers leading Milwaukee by the slimmest of margins. Newcombe, without his best stuff and suffering from a cold, gutted it out for 7.1 innings. He allowed six runs, but the Dodgers scored eight, hitting five home runs. It wasn't pretty, but Don Newcombe finally won a big outing — and the Dodgers took their second straight pennant.

Spahn

CRYING IN BASEBALL

In 1956, there were few tougher men in baseball than Warren Spahn. The Braves lefty had hurled 2,663 innings from 1946–55, a full season's worth more than any other pitcher. He was also a combat veteran, having enlisted in the U.S. Army and earned a Bronze Star in the Battle of the Bulge, the bloodiest conflagration of World War II. He was the last person you would expect to see crying on a baseball field — and yet that's exactly what happened on Sept. 29, 1956, when Spahn suffered a loss that "was the death knell of Milwaukee's pennant hopes," as Robert Creamer wrote.

With his Braves up on Brooklyn by half a game, Spahn had to win or the Dodgers would clinch at least a tie for the pennant. The Braves took a 1-0 lead over St. Louis with a first-inning homer. In the sixth inning, though, Spahn lost the no-hitter, shutout and lead all in a span of two batters. The game went into extras tied, 1-1.

In the top of the 12th, Milwaukee oddly ordered the batter *before* Spahn to sacrifice, bringing the pitcher to the plate with the winning run at second. He flied out for the second out, and the Braves were held. Heading into the bottom of the 12th, Spahn had recorded 22 outs in the air while allowing two hits in 11 frames. But Stan Musial got the best of him, doubling to right. When a hot smash skipped off the glove of third baseman Eddie Mathews, Musial scored the walk-off run. With the pennant having slipped from Milwaukee's grasp, Spahn "came off the mound defeated and crying," Creamer wrote. Even baseball's toughest man had his breaking point.

Mickey Lolich

1972 AL EAST

In the spring of 1972, for the first time, all Major League games were canceled by a players' strike. The labor dispute was settled on April 13, but each team had already lost between six and nine scheduled games, which wouldn't be made up. As a result, different clubs ended up playing different numbers of games. "I don't like that uneven number of games," Detroit outfielder Jim Northrup complained on Opening Day. "I hope nobody wins or loses the pennant by half a game." But that is indeed what would happen — and it was, ironically, Northrup's Tigers who ended up winning the AL East by that exact margin.

Earl Weaver's Baltimore Orioles were the class of the division for most of the season, holding first place for at least part of each month — except, alas, October, as they ended the season on a 3-8 skid. The Red Sox, on the other hand, bided their time before finally charging hard to take over the AL East lead in September. But they too, blew it in the end, dropping three of their last four games, including two key games in Detroit. The Yankees, by contrast, were never in first place for a single day, although they were just half a game out on Sept. 13. But they, too, collapsed, ending the season on a five-game losing streak. With each of their three competitors shooting themselves in the foot, the Tigers managed to swoop in and steal the title by winning five of their last six.

Aparicio (sliding)

RUNNING OUT OF TIME

With three days left in the '72 season, the Red Sox visited Tiger Stadium for an all-important series. Whichever team won two of the three games would become the AL East champ. In the first game, the Sox appeared to break through when Carl Yastrzemski smacked an apparent RBI triple off the center-field fence. But Luis Aparicio, while rounding third base, slipped and fell on wet grass. He was forced to return to third — where, to his dismay, he found Yastrzemski arriving simultaneously. With two runners on third, Yaz was called out, killing the rally. The Sox would drop the game, 4-1. The next day, Boston sent ace Luis Tiant to the mound and grabbed a 1-0 lead in the first inning, but squandered the lead. Tiant took the loss when the go-ahead runs to score on an error in the bottom of the seventh. Even by Red Sox standards, it seemed a particularly cruel way to lose a pennant: a baserunning snafu by the man Yastrzemski called "the best base runner the game had ever seen."

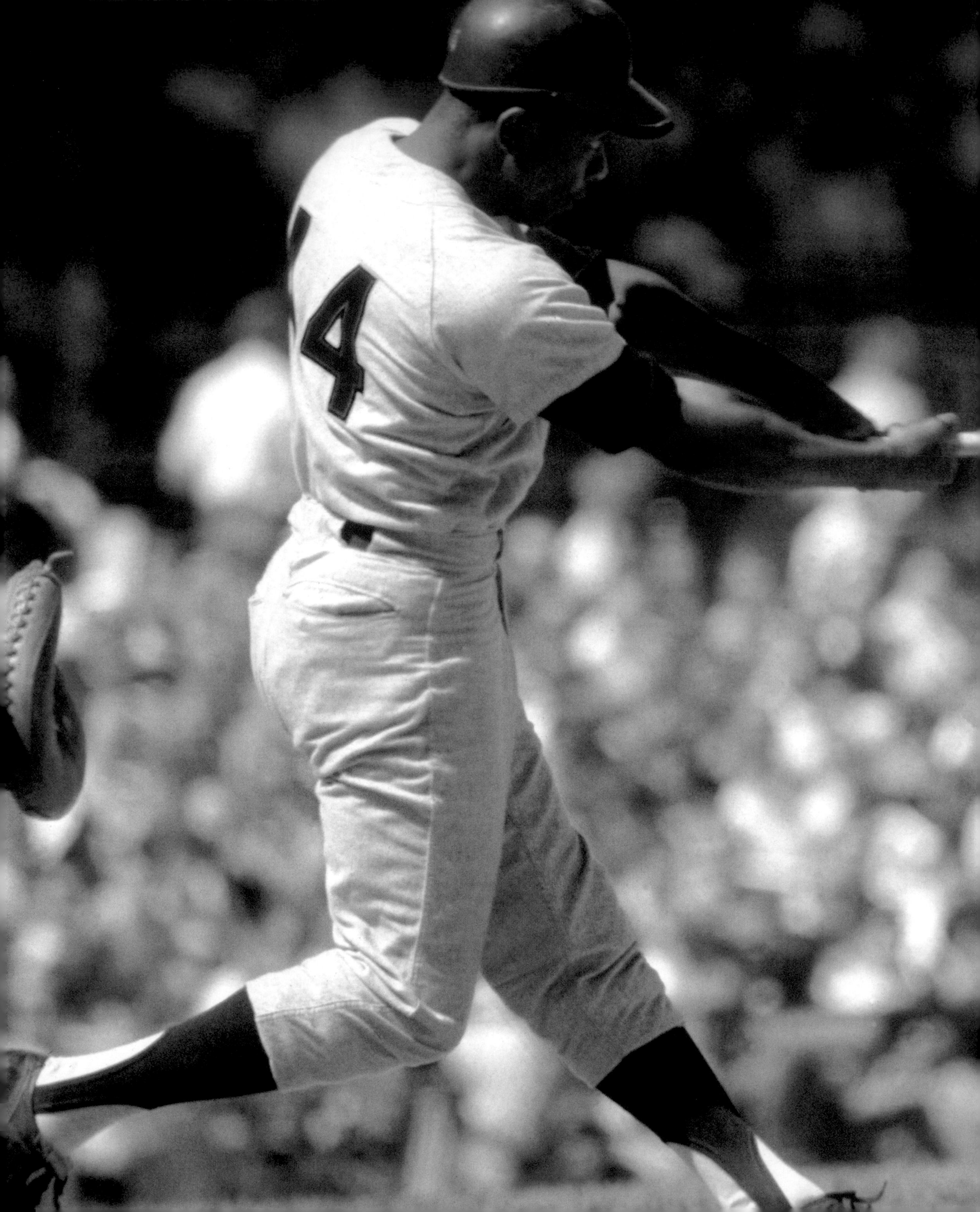

1969 NL WEST

By the start of September 1969, the NL West lead had already changed hands 19 times. The Giants, Dodgers and Reds were within half a game of first place, with the Braves two back, and Houston still holding out hope at 4.5 games behind. The hectic race in the West, coupled with an almost equally exciting chase in the NL East, was a boon for the new divisional playoff system.

"It's going to take about a 10-game winning streak by whoever wins it," Braves slugger Hank Aaron told *Sports Illustrated* in late September. Hammerin' Hank proved prophetic, for almost on the day that he uttered those words, his Braves began a 10-game winning streak that culminated in a division-clinching victory on Sept. 30.

Aaron himself helped lead the charge, batting .357 during the season's final week.

That performance was remarkable considering Aaron played out the final weeks of the season with bone chips and irregular calcium deposits that caused him excruciating back pain. "I'd come out of the lineup if it weren't for the pennant race," he said. "Sometimes I resort to sleeping pills to get any rest." The pain was so much to bear that he publicly contemplated retirement, but the ferocious late-season surge seemed to change his mind. "I've never admitted this before," Aaron said after smacking career homer No. 550 on Sept. 10, "but I'd like to go for Babe Ruth's home run record."

Phil Niekro

SIBLING RIVALRY

With an 8-17 record, 24-year-old Joe Niekro was nobody's idea of an ace — not in 1969, anyway. But on Sept. 26, Joe and the Padres faced the first-place Braves, and who better to defeat Atlanta's 22-game winner Phil Niekro than his little brother? After all, Joe had bested Phil, 1-0, in a classic game three months earlier. It appeared that Joe might pull off another upset when his Padres took a 3-0 lead, but an Orlando Cepeda grand slam soon drove him from the game. Big Brother Phil, meanwhile, stymied the Padres with his famous knuckleball, leaving in the ninth inning having surrendered just two earned runs. The Braves went on to win both the game and the division title, but it was Joe who had the last laugh. In nine career starts against Phil, Joe would go 5-4 and also hit his only career home run.

THREE'S COMPANY

Perhaps the emblematic day of the crazy 1969 NL West race came on Sept. 17, when three different teams held first place at a different time before the clock struck midnight. When the San Francisco Giants woke up that morning in the Bay Area they were half a game ahead of both Los Angeles and Atlanta. But Giants ace Gaylord Perry lost a nail-biter that afternoon to Houston, dropping San Francisco's record to 82-67. The Dodgers, at 81-66, were now in first place, percentage points ahead of the other two teams. But later that evening at Chavez Ravine, the Dodgers dropped a thriller to the Braves on Hank Aaron's 12th-inning homer. That meant Atlanta, at 83-67, was top dog in the division — at least for that moment. The Braves would lose and re-gain the lead all over again before completing their West Coast trip.

Wilhelm

GOLDEN OLDIE

Trailing the Reds by two games in the standings, mired in fourth place in the tightly-packed NL West and anxious to improve their train wreck of a bullpen, the Braves made what seemed to be a desperation move on Sept. 8, 1969: They traded for a reliever who, at age 46, was the oldest player in the Major Leagues by a margin of six years — and was also older than six of the 12 *managers* in the NL.

But of course, Hoyt Wilhelm was no ordinary reliever. The Georgia resident and future Hall of Famer pitched in eight games for the Braves, winning two, saving four others and allowing just one run all month. Although he was crucial in helping the Braves pull out the NL West title, Wilhelm's late arrival made him ineligible for the NLCS — in which the Braves were swept by the surging Mets.

VACUUM CLEANER

Poor Bob Didier. As if being a 20-year-old rookie backstop in the thick of a pennant race wasn't tough enough, he had to learn to catch two different Hall of Fame knuckleballs — Phil Niekro's downward-breaking flutterer, and Hoyt Wilhelm's maddening delivery, which, Didier said, "jumps a lot of different ways." On Sept. 30, all three men performed admirably in Atlanta's dramatic 3-2 pennant-clinching win over Cincinnati. Niekro pitched seven innings, struck out six, walked just one, and went 2 for 2 at the plate. Wilhelm whiffed three in two scoreless, high-pressure innings. And perhaps most impressive of all, Didier made it through the afternoon without allowing a single wild pitch or passed ball.

CHAPTER 5

CONTROVERSIAL FINISHES

1908 Chicago Cubs

1908 NL

The rough-and-tumble 1908 NL pennant chase featured the profane John McGraw, the angelic Christy Mathewson, the conniving Johnny Evers, the admirable Honus Wagner, the unlucky Fred Merkle, the flamboyant Mike Donlin and newcomer Harry Coveleski. There were spikings, spitballs, brawls, incompetent umpires and hurlers who pitched with torn labrums.

After a seesaw summer, "the entire season came down to the arbitrary enforcement of a law," historian Steven Goldman wrote. Indeed, umpire Hank O'Day's handling of the Merkle game ranks among the sport's biggest controversies.

Baseball in 1908, Goldman wrote, "was not a matter of sport but of survival." The three teams involved in the pennant chase — the Cubs, Giants and Pirates — were alive until their last game of the season. Pittsburgh held first place for most of July, part of August and even a few days in October. Having reeled off a 13-1 streak, the Pirates had outright possession of first place on the morning of their final game — but after they lost, everything came down to the Cubs and Giants. Chicago had gotten off to a terrific start, holding the league lead into July, before the Giants wrested it away. But the Cubs persevered through a remarkable spate of injuries to end the season on a 23-4-2 run, catching up to the other two teams — and setting up a dramatic finish that would go down in history.

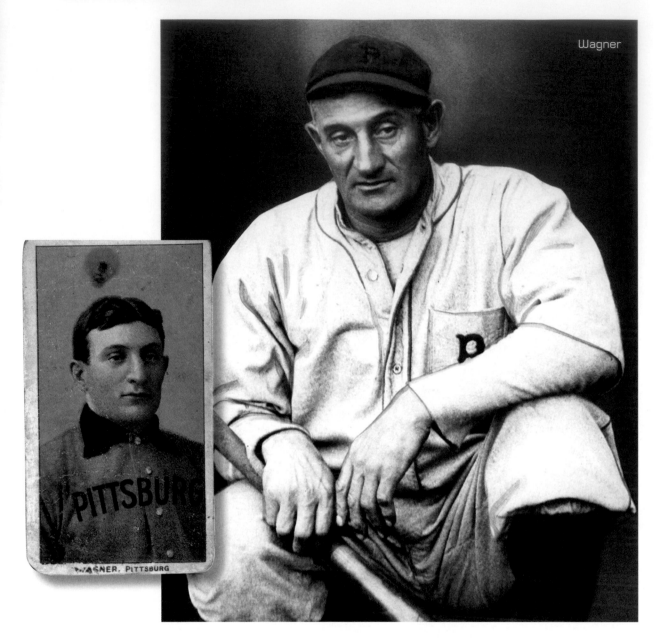

Wagner

ODD COUPLE

The Pirates and Giants stayed in the 1908 race until the end largely because each club possessed one of the two best hitters in the league. But the Pirates' Honus Wagner, the NL batting champ at .354, and the Giants' Mike Donlin, the runner-up at .334, could not have been more different.

Donlin — called "Turkey Mike" because of the way he strutted — was "a flamboyant playboy and partygoer who always had a handshake for everyone he met," wrote his biographer. A scar from an old knife fight ran down his left cheek. A charming rogue, he married Mabel Hite, the era's most glamorous Broadway starlet, and quit baseball after 1908 to star with her in Vaudeville. During his final season, Donlin drove the Giants with 30 steals, 13 triples and 106 RBI.

A friendly and unassuming man, Wagner differed from Donlin in every way. In a year when league-wide batting reached historic lows, "The Flying Dutchman" turned in Major League–leading figures in slugging percentage (.542), steals (53), doubles (39), triples (19), hits (201) and RBI (109), among many other categories. "In my opinion," said Sam Crawford, Ty Cobb's longtime teammate, "the greatest all-around player who ever lived was Honus Wagner."

Merkle

MERKLE'S MISTAKE

The Giants and Cubs were knotted, 1-1, in the bottom of the ninth at New York's Polo Grounds on Sept. 23, 1908, when 19-year-old Giants rookie Fred Merkle, making his first start, singled to put runners at first and third. The next batter also singled, apparently driving in the winning run from third. Since it was customary for fans to exit the ballpark through the playing field, the players sprinted for their center-field clubhouse to escape the throng. What happened next has never been entirely clear. The Cubs' Johnny Evers realized that Merkle had not touched second — and could therefore still be forced out to end the inning, negating the run. Amid the sea of fans, Evers called for the ball. The throw, however, was intercepted by Giants coach Joe McGinnity, who hurled the ball deep into the crowd. Meanwhile, Merkle went back to touch second base, but it was too late. The Cubs somehow found a baseball and stepped on second. Umpire Hank O'Day called Merkle out and officially ruled the game a tie. Infamy would haunt Fred Merkle, although he had been tripped up by a rule that was almost never enforced. His surname became synonymous with stupidity. "I wished," he once said, "that a large, roomy and comfortable hole would open up and swallow me."

Brown

CONTROVERSY REIGNS

The disputed Fred Merkle game became the talk of the nation. Although officially a 1-1 tie, both the Giants and Cubs argued that they should be awarded an outright victory. New York sneered at the absurdity of the technicality, while also noting that the out was almost certainly recorded with the wrong ball. The Cubs, meanwhile, wanted a forfeit, claiming that the New York fans on the field prevented extra innings from being played. The Giants countered that the game would have been halted by darkness anyway. NL President Harry Pulliam backed his umpires, declaring the game a tie, and after an excruciating 18-day delay, the league's Board of Directors agreed, making a decision that Giants skipper John McGraw called "highway robbery." The game would be replayed at the end of the season if necessary. It was, when the Cubs and Giants ended the season tied.

Madness reigned again at the Polo Grounds on Oct. 8. Mobs rushed the gate, and an overflow crowd lined the outfield grass. Thousands who were turned away climbed every telephone pole, fence and hillside that offered a view of the field. It was, at the time, the best-attended game in Major League history. The Giants even offered a $2,500 bribe to umpire Bill Klem. Fortunately, he refused it.

After New York took a 1-0 lead, Mordecai "Three Finger" Brown entered in relief for Chicago, and a dream matchup between Brown and Christy Mathewson materialized. Unfortunately for Giants fans, Mathewson had been worked to the bone down the stretch. He had nothing left. "I'm not fit to pitch today," he told his wife before leaving for the ballpark. The Cubs bludgeoned him for four runs in the third, and with Brown on the mound, that's all Chicago needed. The Cubs won the game, 4-2, and the pennant along with it.

THE REAL GIANT KILLER

"Most people think it was Merkle who lost the 1908 pennant for the Giants," Hall of Fame pitcher Stan Coveleski once told author Larry Ritter. "Well, they're wrong. It was Harry Coveleski. He was just a rookie, but he beat the Giants three times in the last week of the season." Stan was right to speak up on behalf of his big brother. For in the final days of the 1908 campaign, Harry won the nickname "The Giant Killer" by manhandling New York — still reeling from the Merkle madness — and almost single-handedly eliminating the club from the pennant race.

A tough lefty whose ability to throw a baseball had enabled him to escape the coal mines of northeastern Pennsylvania, the 22-year-old Harry won 22 games for Class-B Lancaster in 1908, earning him a call-up to the Phillies. On Sept. 29, he earned the third victory of his Major League career when he shut out the Giants, 7-0. Two days later he beat them, 6-2. Two days after that, he beat them yet again, 3-2. Remarkably, those three games were the only ones the Giants lost in the season's final two weeks, and they were enough to drop the team into a tie with the Cubs and force a replay of the Merkle game. When the Giants lost the title they didn't blame Merkle for their misfortune, but Coveleski. "Coveleski beating us three times in one week surely wasn't Merkle's fault," outfielder Fred Snodgrass said.

1965 NL

The 1965 National League pennant race seemingly had everything. It had one of the most celebrated and competitive rivalries in baseball — the longtime feud between the Dodgers and Giants. It had controversy, with Juan Marichal and John Roseboro facing off in the most famous fight in the sport's history. It had obstacles, with one team's best hitter injured all season and the other team's best pitcher suspended during the stretch drive. It had tension, as San Francisco and Los Angeles went from Aug. 15 through Sept. 12 without being separated by more than 2.5 games in the standings. And most memorably, thanks to Sandy Koufax, it had the greatest sustained clutch performance any Major League pitcher has ever turned in during a pennant race.

As the summer wound down, it seemed as if more teams than just the Dodgers and Giants would join the party. On Sept. 1, three other clubs — Cincinnati, Pittsburgh and Milwaukee — were also within 2.5 games of first place. The Pirates were the first contender to fade, dropping out of the race almost immediately after the calendar turned to September. The Braves were the next to fall, ending the season on a gruesome 7-14 skid. Next came the Reds, who suddenly sank like a stone after being just half a game out on Sept. 10. The pennant, then, would be decided between Los Angeles and San Francisco — and oh, what a contest it would be.

UGLY TURN

Things were always contentious between the Dodgers and Giants, but they were never as violent as on Aug. 22, 1965, when the two clubs faced off at Candlestick Park with Los Angeles leading by 1.5 games. Earlier in the game, the Giants' Matty Alou had struck the glove of Dodgers catcher John Roseboro on his backswing — a deliberate attempt, Roseboro felt, to injure him. Making matters worse, Juan Marichal threw at two Dodgers batters in the first inning. Since Los Angeles starter Sandy Koufax was "constitutionally incapable of throwing at anyone's head," Roseboro knew retaliation was up to him.

When Marichal came to bat, Roseboro whizzed a return throw to Koufax by the batter's ear. "He protested," Roseboro wrote in his autobiography. "I went to hit him with a punch and he hit me with his bat." Marichal ripped off Roseboro's mask and whaled away with his bat. Marichal got in three swings — one of which struck Roseboro flush on the head and caused him to lose vision when blood flooded his eyes — before the melee was broken up. "Willie Mays sat by my side," Roseboro recalled, "cradling my head in his hands and crying." Roseboro was rushed to the hospital and his injuries sidelined him for two games.

Marichal was suspended for eight playing dates. In effect, he missed one start and had another pushed back. NL President Warren Giles conceded that he had taken "underlying currents" — that is, Roseboro's ear-buzzing throw — into consideration. With the teams so near each other in the standings, Giles feared having a suspension determine the outcome of the pennant race. Marichal's missed start was taken by Gaylord Perry, who was roughed up in a loss. It's unlikely that was the difference-maker, though, as the Dodgers ended up winning the pennant by two games.

Marichal swings at Roseboro

Koufax

SWEET LOU

In 1962, Tommy Davis had driven in 153 runs, and in 1963, he had won his second straight NL batting crown. In 1965, he hoped to lead Los Angeles to a world title, but that dream hit a major bump when, on May 1, Davis broke his leg in horrific fashion sliding into second base. His season was over, and his career would never be the same. The Dodgers, meanwhile, had to scramble to replace their top hitter.

The club called up 30-year-old career Minor Leaguer Lou Johnson, who they had acquired from the Tigers, along with $10,000, the previous April in exchange for pitcher Larry Sherry. The anonymous outfielder, playing with his eighth Major League organization since being signed as an amateur free agent by the Yankees in 1953, surprised everyone by batting .346 in his first 33 games after replacing Davis. "Sweet Lou" gave the team a much needed morale boost before eventually slumping down the stretch. Still, his contributions were noted, with Johnson even receiving consideration for the NL MVP Award.

Even though Johnson couldn't keep up his torrid pace over the duration of the 1965 campaign, he did make sure that the injured Davis got that coveted ring when he hit a dramatic homer to win Game 7 of the World Series. Having batted .296 during the taut seven-game Fall Classic against the Minnesota Twins, Johnson made the most of his walk-on cameo in Hollywood.

ONE MAN ARMY

Embroiled in a tight pennant race, there is no better weapon to have than someone like Sandy Koufax. The legendary left-hander won his second Cy Young Award in 1965 and, more importantly, won the pennant for Los Angeles all but singlehandedly. On Sept. 9, Koufax pitched a perfect game. On Sept. 18, he twirled a four-hit shutout. On Sept. 25, it was a five-hit shutout with 12 strikeouts — one of which was his 350th of the season, breaking the modern record. On Sept. 29, he threw a two-hit shutout with 13 K's. And finally, on Oct. 2, Koufax took the mound on two days' rest for a potential pennant-clinching game — and of course spun another masterpiece, defeating the Braves, 2-1, while whiffing 13 batters yet again. Miraculously, he did all this with a sore and arthritic left arm. The injury would eventually end Koufax's dynastic run through the NL. "If his elbow hurts him," Cincinnati Manager Dick Sisler quipped, "it certainly isn't between the first and ninth innings."

Finally, on Oct. 2, Koufax took the mound on two days' rest for a potential pennant-clinching game — and of course spun another masterpiece, defeating the Braves, 2-1, while whiffing 13 batters yet again.

1920 AL

"The baseball sky was black and gloomy," *Baseball Magazine*'s W.A. Phelon wrote about the end of the 1920 season. "The great gambling scandal had made the fans sore, sullen and suspicious." Indeed, the revelation of the "Black Sox" scandal from the previous World Series had cast a cloud over the game, and baseball would have to work hard to regain the trust of its loyal fans. That process started with the 1920 AL pennant race, a three-team contest that featured as many outlandish storylines as the dime novels that were the era's dominant literature.

In Chicago, eight guilty "Black Sox" were suspended and disgraced, which only made the team's remaining innocent players seem that much more admirable as they fought on. In New York, the game's greatest idol outdid even his own previous exploits. In Cleveland, a team rallied around the memory of a fallen hero. Even if disillusioned fans may have considered turning away from baseball, the excitement of the pennant pursuit simply wouldn't let them. "The American League pennant race enters its closing three weeks with no signs of a break on the part of any of the three clubs," *The New York Times* wrote on Sept. 13. "Nothing in sight can be considered as giving any of the contenders any marked advantage over the others."

Speaker

Ruth

Instead of slapping at the ball with all his weight on his front foot, Ruth stood back and slugged, using balance and power to tally 54 homers in 1920 — a total nearly double his own single-season record, and higher than that of every other *team* in the league.

STEAL OF THE CENTURY

On Jan. 5, 1920, Boston Red Sox Owner Harry Frazee sold baseball's top player, pitcher-outfielder Babe Ruth, to the Yankees for a whopping $125,000 plus a $300,000 loan. Frazee needed the money, but also viewed the transaction as addition by subtraction. "Despite his 29 home runs, the Red Sox finished sixth last year," Frazee said. "What the Boston fans want … is a winning team, rather than a one-man team that finishes in sixth place."

The Yankees, one of five teams that had never won a pennant, were transformed. Ruth approached hitting unlike anyone before him. Instead of slapping at the ball with all his weight on his front foot, Ruth stood back and slugged, using balance and power to tally 54 home runs in 1920 — a total nearly double his own single-season record, and higher than that of every other *team* in the league. Crowds loved it, and the Yankees drew twice as many fans as they ever had before. After spending parts of June, July, August and September in first place, they fell three games short in the final standings. But Ruth had erased any doubts about his ability to be part of a winning team, and the Yankees were on their way to building the game's most enduring dynasty.

DARK DAY

With storm clouds roiling over the Polo Grounds on Aug. 16, 1920, the first-place Indians and the second-place Yankees faced off. Foul-tempered submariner Carl Mays took the hill for New York. "He intimidated batters," longtime opponent George Uhle remembered. In the fifth inning Ray Chapman, Cleveland's shortstop, dug in and, as usual, crowded the plate. Mays threw an inside pitch, and Chapman froze. Perhaps it was too dark to see the soiled ball, or perhaps he panicked. Either way, the ball smacked Chapman squarely in the temple and he crumpled to the ground. The ball bounced so far that the Yankees thought it had hit Chapman's bat. Mays even fielded the ball and threw to first. Meanwhile, blood was spurting from Chapman's ear. He was rushed to the hospital, but it was too late; Chapman died the next morning. He remains the only player killed on a Major League diamond. The reaction against Mays was instantaneous and vicious. Ty Cobb demanded his banishment from baseball. "I would give anything if I could undo what has happened," Mays said. He was eventually forgiven, but Chapman's death prompted a call for greater safety regulations, including keeping a clean ball in play at all times.

Sewell

ROOKIE PITCHERS TO THROW A SHUTOUT IN THE WORLD SERIES			
PLAYER	TEAM	YEAR	SCORE
Babe Adams	Pirates	1909	8-0
Walter Mails	**Indians**	**1920**	**1-0**
Gene Bearden	Indians	1948	2-0

A SILVER LINING

Ray Chapman's death on Aug. 17, 1920, plunged the Cleveland Indians into a state of mourning. They could not, however, afford to grieve without distraction since they were locked in a tight pennant race. Cleveland was in first place with two teams hot on their heels, and they were now without a shortstop. They first turned to the team's utility infielder, Harry Lunte, but he batted just .197. On Sept. 10, the club acquired rookie Joe Sewell, who had a .289 batting average for Class-A New Orleans but had never even *seen* a Major League game, much less played in one. Sewell proved up to the task, though, raking at a .329 clip with an on-base percentage of .413 over the season's final 22 games. Sewell would enjoy a stellar 14-year career and be elected to the Hall of Fame. Ordinarily a player added as late as Sewell would have been ineligible for the World Series, but the Indians' opponents, the Brooklyn Robins, allowed the rule to be waived due to Chapman's death.

But he was not the only rookie who proved vital during the pennant race. The Indians also needed a left-handed pitcher. "Get me anyone who wasn't here when Chappie got it," Manager Tris Speaker ordered. "Get me that big Mails from Portland." Southpaw Walter Mails, nicknamed "Duster" for his frequent brushback pitches, arrived at the end of August from the Pacific Coast League. Armed with a blazing fastball and superb control, the 25-year-old went 8-0 with a spectacular 1.48 ERA, and tossed 15.2 frames of shutout ball in the World Series. "An ominous cloud seemed to gather over Cleveland's pennant prospects," *Baseball Magazine* said. "But in the hour when that cloud seemed darkest it developed the proverbial silver lining and the name of that silver lining was Walter Mails."

CLEAN SOX

In 1919, seven members of the Chicago White Sox accepted money from gamblers to intentionally lose the World Series. Although the powerhouse club's lackluster performance immediately drew whispers that the Fall Classic hadn't been on the level, the "Black Sox's" chicanery officially remained a secret for nearly a year. But on Sept. 27, 1920, with the Sox once again in the hunt for the pennant, the scandal blew sky-high when one of the gamblers confessed all the sordid details to a reporter. It was the biggest scandal in baseball history, and eight players — the seven guilty men plus third baseman Buck Weaver, who had known about the fix but failed to report it — were immediately suspended.

There were calls for the rest of the Major League season to be canceled, too, but Commissioner Kenesaw Mountain Landis ordered games to proceed as scheduled. That was a tall order for the undermanned "Clean Sox," who were just half a game behind in the standings with three games left in the season, but suddenly found themselves without eight of their best players.

THE AFTERMATH

The White Sox took what must have seemed like an interminably long train ride to St. Louis for the final series of 1920. The fallout from the team's tainted loss to the Reds in the 1919 World Series must have exceeded the fears of even the most straitlaced players on the ballcub. And the hammer could hardly have come down at a less opportune time, with Commissioner Kenesaw Mountain Landis handing down his landmark ruling — banning the eight players involved for life — just before the season-ending series versus the Browns. But, even with their roster decimated, the remaining players still had a job to do. Only 1.5 games behind, they still had a shot at first place. They needed to sweep St. Louis and hope first-place Cleveland went 2-2 in the last matchup of the campaign. The Indians did in fact go 2-2, but the Sox failed to hold up their end of the bargain. In their first game after getting off the train, Chicago took an early lead, but then turned around and gave up five runs in the third. The game, and effectively the season, was over as Cleveland clinched the pennant.

> Even with their roster decimated, the remaining players still had a job to do. Only 1.5 games behind, they still had a shot at first place. They needed to sweep St. Louis and hope first-place Cleveland went 2-2.

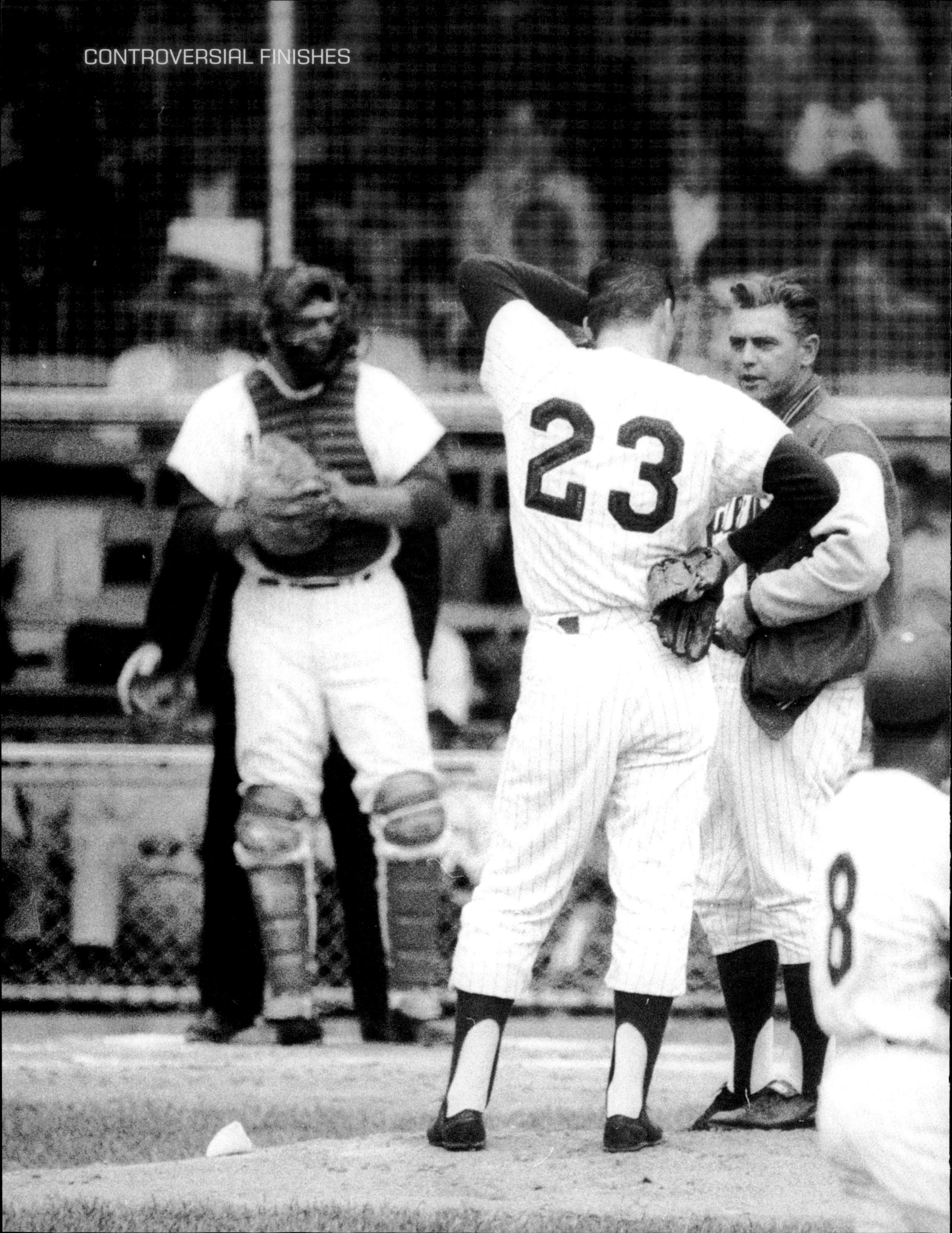
23
8

Phillies Manager Gene Mauch (right), Dennis Bennett (23) in a game against the Cardinals

1964 NL

In St. Louis, the 1964 pennant race is remembered as a great comeback. In Philadelphia, it's remembered as the most painful collapse in baseball history. In Cincinnati, it seems to be remembered hardly at all — which is strange, for the Reds were also in the three-team race until the final day of the season.

The standings were a jumble until late July, when the Phillies began to pull away. They built up their lead slowly, until, on Sept. 18, it stood at a seemingly insurmountable 6.5 games. That's when the infamous collapse began, but of course, for a collapse to mean anything, another team has to take advantage of it. "Everybody talks about the collapse of the Phillies in 1964," Cardinals infielder Dick Groat told writer Danny Peary. "But don't forget how good we played down the stretch." St. Louis played very well indeed, ending the season on a 38-11 run. Even as late as Sept. 21, a *Sports Illustrated* headline called the Cards' streak a "futile surge," but they proved the doubters wrong, capturing the pennant on the final day.

The Cards entered that last day tied — not with the Phillies, but with the Frank Robinson–led Reds, who were on a 13-4 streak of their own. But, Cincinnati ace Jim Maloney declined to start the season finale on three days' rest, preferring to save himself for a potential playoff game. Journeyman John Tsitouris got the start instead, and was clobbered, 10-0, by the already eliminated Phillies.

Brock (sliding)

CHANGE OF SCENERY

In 1964, with the Chicago Cubs wallowing near the bottom of the National League standings, Wrigley Field's frustrated bleacherites began to lustily shower boos upon their right fielder, Lou Brock, a gifted athlete who had yet to maximize his full potential on the baseball diamond. "Brock fielded poorly, hit only in the mid-.200s and was rarely given the green light to show off his strongest baseball talent — base stealing," *Sports Illustrated*'s Peter Carry wrote.

LOU BROCK'S STATS BEFORE AND AFTER 1964 TRADE							
TEAM	G	R	H	3B	HR	SB	AVG
CHI	52	30	54	2	2	10	.251
STL	103	81	146	9	12	33	.348

Shipped to St. Louis for ace hurler Ernie Broglio at the June 15 trading deadline, the 24-year-old Brock erupted into a completely different player. He batted .348 as a Cardinal, upped his season totals to 200 hits and 111 runs, and, after being unshackled, swiped bases at an impressive rate.

With Brock at the top of the lineup, St. Louis ultimately won the pennant thanks to one of the savviest trade-deadline deals ever made. "The Cardinals," catcher Tim McCarver later said, "didn't know they were getting such a dynamic package."

BURNED OUT

Perhaps all one needs to know about Phillies Manager Gene Mauch's performance in the 1964 pennant race is that when ESPN's Rob Neyer wrote *Rob Neyer's Big Book of Baseball Blunders*, Mauch's photo graced the cover. In history's most infamous example of managerial strategy gone awry, Mauch continued to start aces Jim Bunning and Chris Short on almost no rest down the stretch in '64, even as their performances indicated it was a bad idea. Mauch's ill-advised gambit helped the Phils blow a 6.5-game lead with only a dozen games left in the season.

Mauch refused to use talented rookie Rick Wise, a future All-Star who spent September riding the pine. He also benched veteran Art Mahaffey, a 12-game winner, because of a personal squabble with the pitcher. "He wouldn't give Mahaffey the ball," Bunning complained years later. "There was no reason for him not to."

Instead of letting Mahaffey and Wise do their parts, Mauch rode Bunning and Short to the point of breakdown. On Sept. 16, Bunning started on two days' rest and was rocked for six runs. On Sept. 27, he started again on two days' rest and gave up seven runs. On Sept. 30, it was two days' rest once more, and six more runs surrendered.

Short, meanwhile, was used on three days' rest throughout September before making two starts on two days' rest — and losing both. The latter came in the opener of a vital three-game series with the hard-charging Cardinals. "Short … was the Phillies pitcher we were scared to death of," St. Louis's Dick Groat later said. "When we beat him we felt we had a chance to sweep them." The Cards did sweep, knocking the Phillies into third place. "Future generations will be told this incredible horror story," Larry Merchant wrote in the *Philadelphia Daily News*. "Children will shriek, adults will shiver, managers will faint."

Allen

NO COMEBACK KIDS

By Oct. 2, the Phillies had almost completed their historic collapse. The writing was on the wall after a devastating 10-game losing streak, but the dispirited squad still had a mathematical chance to win the pennant if they could get back on track at the same time that the Cardinals faltered. Ace lefty Chris Short — starting on three days' rest this time — turned in his best performance in ages in the team's penultimate game, yet the Phils still fell behind to Cincinnati, 3-0. Just five outs shy of official elimination, Philadelphia began to show some fight, tying the game on an eighth-inning triple by hard-hitting rookie Dick Allen. The Phils won, 4-3, but their elation was brief, as they were eliminated two days later even after another win over the Reds. On the gloomy flight home from Cincinnati, players began to worry that an irate throng of Philly fans would show up at the airport to jeer the team as they disembarked. "I want to be the first one off," Manager Gene Mauch told his players. "You guys didn't lose it. I did."

CHAPTER 6

AMAZING COMEBACKS

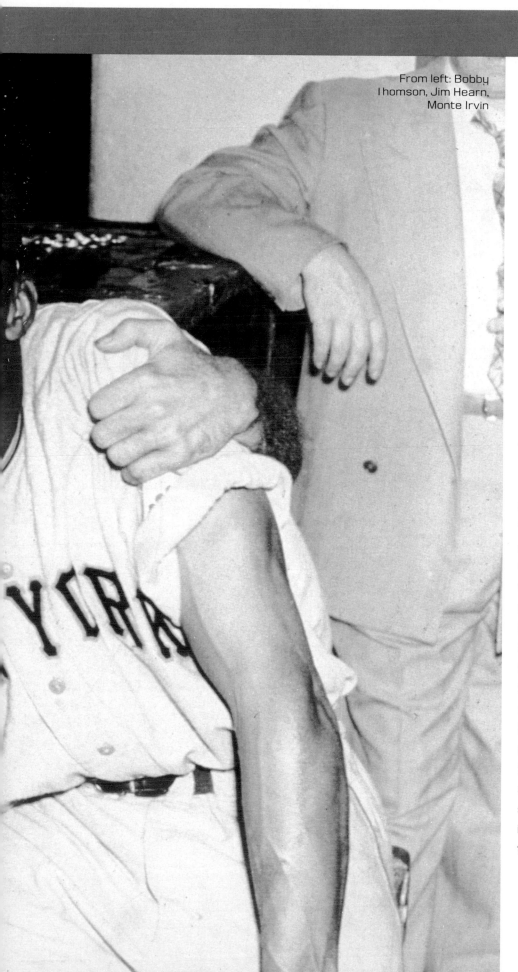

From left: Bobby Thomson, Jim Hearn, Monte Irvin

1951 NL

The 1951 NL race had it all. It featured a huge blown lead — Brooklyn led by 13 games on Aug. 12 — and one Giant comeback. It featured a fierce rivalry. It featured a Giants manager (Leo Durocher) who had won a pennant as a Dodger, and a Dodgers skipper (Charlie Dressen) who had won a flag playing for New York. It featured the finest game ever played by Jackie Robinson and the debut of a 20-year-old named Willie Mays. It featured, in a four-day span, not one but *two* of the most incredible regular-season games ever. And it featured the homer that remains the most famous to date.

Great races shock people by heating up when each club's destiny seems secure. In 1951, it began on Aug. 9, when Brooklyn swept the Giants and taunted its rivals through the thin walls that separated their clubhouses at Ebbets Field. But from that point forward, New York hardly lost a game, going 37-8 to pull even in the standings as the Dodgers went 27-23. Brooklyn didn't exactly choke, but it did allow New York to snatch away the title at the last second. "The art of fiction is dead," columnist Red Smith wrote after the race's climax. "Reality has strangled invention. Only the utterly impossible, the inexpressibly fantastic, can ever be plausible again."

Mays

Dressen

NEW KID IN TOWN

Six weeks into the 1951 season, the Giants — tied for fifth place in the National League with a mediocre 17-19 record — looked like anything but World Series contenders. But they had a secret weapon: One of the greatest prospects anyone had ever seen was cooling his heels at Triple-A Minneapolis. On May 25 — just a few weeks past his 20th birthday — Willie Mays was handed the Giants' center field job after tearing up the American Association to the tune of a .477 batting average, eight home runs and a .799 slugging percentage.

The anointed savior got off to a rough start, going 0 for 12. He finally collected his first hit — a homer off the legendary Warren Spahn — in his 13th at-bat, and never looked back. Mays finished the year with 20 homers, earning Rookie of the Year honors, and led the Giants to the pennant.

DORMANT, NOT DEAD

When a good ballclub storms out to a seemingly insurmountable lead, wise managers will warn their ballplayers not to start popping the champagne until the pennant is officially secured. But on Aug. 9, 1951, after a dominant three-game sweep of New York stretched Brooklyn's lead in the NL to 12.5 games, Dodgers Manager Charlie Dressen gleefully (and ungrammatically) declared, "The Giants is dead!"

Dressen and veteran players Pee Wee Reese, Jackie Robinson and others who should have known better, lit a fire under the Giants by taunting them with victory songs following the game while pounding on the thin wall that separated the two teams' clubhouses. The Giants took note, went an unbelievable 39-9 over the remainder of the season, including the three-game playoff, and by Oct. 3 it was Dressen's Dodgers who were dead.

On May 25 — just a few weeks past his 20th birthday — Willie Mays was handed the Giants' center field job after tearing up the American Association.

Robinson

CAREER DAY

Often the center of attention during his landmark career with the Dodgers, it's surprising that Jackie Robinson's finest baseball moment has nearly been forgotten, overshadowed by the dramatic playoff games that followed it.

On Sept. 30, 1951, with the pennant on the line, Brooklyn and Philadelphia played one of the most intense and memorable games in NL history, and Robinson was the star among stars, making game-altering plays in the field and at the plate. It was a must-win for Brooklyn, which hoped to stay even with New York and force a three-game playoff. The Bums' hopes all but disappeared when Philly took a 6-1 lead, but Brooklyn eventually tied it, 8-8, in the eighth. Things again appeared grim for Brooklyn when Philadelphia loaded the bases with two outs in the 12th. Phillies first baseman Eddie Waitkus lashed a liner to right-center for a potential walk-off single, but Robinson saved the day with a once-in-a-lifetime snag. "He did it with as self-punishing and spectacular a play as the 31,755 attending fans … will ever see," sportswriter Dick Young wrote. "Robby diving face-first speared the ball an instant before he hit the ground. As he struck, his elbow dug into his stomach and he lay there in a crumpled heap."

Robinson remained motionless for what seemed like an eternity before he rose and everyone at Shibe Park saw that, miraculously, he held onto the ball. He then smashed a game-winning homer in the 14th to give Brooklyn a 9-8 victory and square the club with New York. "Of all the pictures left in memory," Pulitzer Prize–winning sportswriter Red Smith penned, "the one that will always flash back shows [Robinson] stretched at full length in the insubstantial twilight, the unconquerable doing the impossible."

JUBILATION

All of New York seemed to be talking about the three-game playoff between the Giants and Dodgers, and much of the nation was captivated, too, as the opening game was the first baseball contest ever telecast from coast to coast. Unbeknownst to viewers, it also previewed coming attractions: The Giants won, 3-1, on a game-winning homer by Bobby Thomson off Ralph Branca.

Brooklyn pummeled New York, 10-0, the next day, bringing the season down to game No. 157 at the Polo Grounds. Each team threw its ace — the Dodgers' Don Newcombe and the Giants' Sal Maglie. In the eighth Brooklyn erupted to take a 4-1 lead. But in the ninth, the Giants had the heart of their order due up. Newcombe, seeming gassed, gave up hits to the first two batters, then got a pop-up before serving up a double. With Bobby Thomson up as the winning run, Dodgers Manager Chuck Dressen called on the pitcher Thomson had beaten 48 hours earlier: Ralph Branca.

In an 0-1 count, Branca tried to waste a fastball high and inside. It was a good pitch, but Thomson put a solid swing on it, parking the ball in the left-field seats for a walk-off homer. "The Giants win the pennant! The Giants win the pennant!" shouted radio announcer Russ Hodges. "They're going crazy! They're going crazy!"

The Dodgers' clubhouse was "like a tomb," Brooklyn's Carl Erskine later said. "[Gil] Hodges quietly put his glove in his locker. Jackie [Robinson] slammed his glove. Dressen ripped his shirt off. Branca plopped down on the steps inside the clubhouse. I was never superstitious, but it seemed like the No. 13 on Ralph's back was jumping out at you."

The Giants
celebrate
clinching the
1951 NL
pennant

THOMSON'S BAT

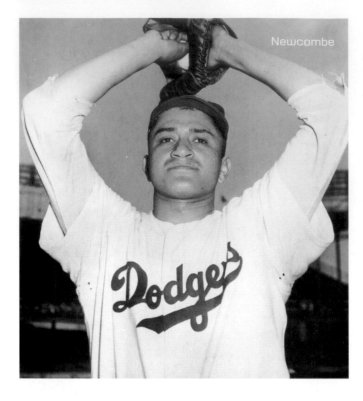

Newcombe

SMALL-TIME ACE

Although he was undeniably an ace by 1951, Dodgers pitcher Don Newcombe had the unflattering reputation of someone who would crumble under the pressure of pitching in important games. As a rookie in 1949, he had lost both of his World Series starts — pitching brilliantly in one and getting shelled in the other. In 1950, he had lost the season's final game with the pennant on the line. In '51, he almost did it again, only to be saved when Jackie Robinson dove to catch a potential game-ending hit.

So Newcombe's performance in the infamous Bobby Thomson game — when he was unable to shut the door in the ninth inning, forcing the Dodgers to bring in Ralph Branca — was chalked up as just another instance of him coming up short when it mattered most. The pattern continued, as Newcombe would pitch three more World Series games over his career and get shellacked in each one. It may have been a simple case of fatigue or overwork, but Newcombe had cemented his reputation as a great pitcher who came up short in the biggest moments.

ONE AND DONE

If you're a pitcher, there is a list of fellow hurlers you never want to join. Dennis Eckersley, Ralph Terry and Mitch Williams were all fine pitchers, but each is chiefly remembered for giving up one of baseball's most famous home runs. On Oct. 3, 1951, 25-year-old Ralph Branca preceded those players, and his career was never the same. Although it's simplistic to peg Bobby Thomson's legendary homer as the cause of Branca's downfall, his numbers before and after the incident are shocking. Before the homer, he was 76-55 with a 3.64 ERA. After, he went 12-12 with a 4.54 mark. "If I had my druthers, I would have gotten him out," Branca told ESPN's Tim Kurkjian. "I haven't dwelled on it. … I'm not going to cry about it. It is what it is. You go forth. You want to go on [and] live your life."

Eckersley, Terry and Williams were fine pitchers, but each is chiefly remembered for giving up one of baseball's most famous home runs. Ralph Branca preceded those players, and his career was never the same.

Branca

Giants fans celebrate
Thomson's pennant-
clinching homer

FRIENDLY HELP

In 2001, a front-page story in *The Wall Street Journal* exposed a shocking secret of the team that had upended the rival Dodgers on Bobby Thomson's longball 50 years earlier. Investigative reporter Josh Prager exposed an elaborate sign-stealing system that may have aided the Giants in mounting their miraculous comeback. These were no mere allegations, either: Prager's well-documented article included admissions of guilt from Giants players.

The scheme was certainly clever. The Giants' clubhouse at the Polo Grounds stood in dead center field, perfect for someone with a telescope to steal the opposing catcher's signs. New York rigged up a buzzer system whereby the telescope snoop could relay signals to the bullpen. There, third-string catcher Sal Yvars would sit next to the buzzer and convey its results to batters. "I'll have a baseball in my hand," Yvars said. "If I hold onto the ball, it's a fastball. If I toss the ball in the air, it's a breaking ball."

Stealing signs is not traditionally considered to be cheating. What made the scheme against the rules was the electrical wiring. Stealing signs *by electronic means*, even then, violated the rules. How much the Giants' chicanery actually helped them, though, is an open question. During their season-ending hot streak, the Giants performed about the same at home (21-4) as on the road (18-4), where presumably no signs were being stolen. But, of course, in a pennant race so tight, all it would have taken was one stolen sign to make a difference. Thomson, asked by Prager whether he knew in advance that Ralph Branca would throw a fastball in that fateful play-off game, hemmed and hawed and was ultimately unable to give a straightforward answer. "My answer is no," Thomson finally managed to say. "I was always proud of that swing."

1942 NL

In an excruciating pennant race in 1941, the veteran Dodgers squeaked past the up-and-coming Cardinals. Finishing just shy of the pennant might have demoralized some clubs, but not St. Louis, which vowed not to let history repeat itself in '42. "The 1942 Cardinals were the greatest club I ever played on," Hall of Fame outfielder Enos Slaughter told writer Donald Honig.

"There was tremendous team play and desire; we felt like we couldn't be beat." It helped, too, that the Cardinals had Stan Musial playing in his first full season.

The Dodgers, though, were still intimidating: They had taken a pennant-winning team and *improved* it. They had four future Hall of Famers in their lineup, a total that didn't include the reigning NL MVP, Dolph

From left: Whitey Kurowski, Marty Marion, Musial, Ray Sanders

Camilli, and the '42 MVP front-runner, Pete Reiser. By early August, Brooklyn held a 10-game lead and was looking like an all-time great club.

But Reiser, who was leading the NL in batting, hits, runs and steals, got hurt on July 19, and the Cardinals seized their chance. While the Dodgers began a solid 35-23 run, the Cardinals reeled off an amazing 43-8 streak that enabled them to take over first place on Sept. 13. Brooklyn recovered to win its final eight games, but it was too late — the Cardinals won 12 of their last 13, and the pennant was theirs. Unlike most, the 1942 race had no goats and no failures. Brooklyn played spectacularly down the stretch. St. Louis simply played better.

Walker Cooper (left), Mort Cooper

BROTHER ACT

Most catchers making their Major League debut are nervous about working with a new pitcher for the first time, not knowing the hurler's tendencies or nuances. Not so, however, for Walker Cooper, who caught his big brother Mort — two years Walker's senior — when he played his first Big League game as a 25-year-old with the St. Louis Cardinals on Sept. 25, 1940.

By 1942, the dynamic sibling duo was not only leading the Cardinals to the league championship, but also serving as the National League's starting battery in the All-Star Game. Walker, recognized as the Majors' top backstop, batted .281 with 32 doubles and seven triples in 125 games played — finishing 11th in NL MVP balloting. Mort, meanwhile, was named 1942 MVP after recording 152 strikeouts and leading the Big Leagues with 22 victories, 10 shutouts, a 1.78 ERA, an 0.987 WHIP and a 2.24 strikeout-to-walk rate. Throughout the long season, the steady, rock-solid Walker guided the high-strung, temperamental Mort — even going so far as to decide when Mort should be removed from games. "He had to be pulled out," Walker said of his big brother, "or he'd hurt the other 24 players."

NEVER THE SAME

In 1942, there was no greater all-around Big Leaguer than Pete Reiser. A true five-tool superstar, the Dodgers' speedy center fielder had burst onto the scene a year earlier, winning the NL batting title at .343 in his first full Big League season. For good measure, he also led the league in doubles, triples, runs and slugging. Through mid-1942 he was even more spectacular, hitting .359 and seemingly running away with his second straight batting crown as the Dodgers jumped out to a seven-game lead. But all that came crashing down — literally — in a July 19 game at second-place St. Louis.

The Dodgers and Cards were tied in the bottom of the 11th when Enos Slaughter crushed a ball to center. Reiser raced back, leapt to make a one-handed catch, and crashed brutally into the unpadded wall. The impact knocked the ball loose, and Slaughter had himself a walk-off, inside-the-park homer. The woozy Reiser was rushed to the hospital, where he was diagnosed with a concussion (later changed to a fractured skull).

Remarkably, Reiser returned to the lineup just six days later even though doctors advised him to sit out the remainder of the season. Sure enough he wasn't the same — in fact, he would never be the same again. Plagued by blurred vision and headaches, Reiser batted just .238 after his return. "Gradually I kept getting weaker and weaker," he later recalled. "I probably shouldn't have played. … There's no question in my mind that by being stubborn, I cost the Dodgers the pennant in 1942."

In future years there were more wall collisions, more injuries, and Reiser ended up having a pedestrian career rather than the Hall of Fame one everyone expected. He did have one group of devoted followers, though: the kids from the Missouri School for the Blind, who, strangely, invited Reiser to speak year after year. "You're our favorite player," the director explained. "Our children here always have problems with walls, and they hear that you have the same problem. They figure you're one of them."

PETE REISER'S CAREER STATS BEFORE AND AFTER HEAD INJURY							
	G	R	H	AVG	HR	RBI	BB
1940–42	320	240	399	.322	27	160	109
1946–52	541	233	387	.272	31	208	234

Durocher

SECOND BEST

If you were the manager of a baseball team and were told before the season that you would go 104-50 and feature a star at each of the eight positions, plus four 15-game winners and baseball's best relief ace — well, you would certainly accept that deal. In 1942, though, all that would have gotten you was second place. Leo Durocher's Brooklyn Dodgers had all the aforementioned qualities and more, but their 104 victories simply weren't good enough to top the Cardinals, who were even more spectacular with 106 wins. "We were hungry," St. Louis's Enos Slaughter said. "Young, talented, confident and hungry. That's a tough combination to beat." No other team has ever won as many games as the Dodgers' 104 and failed to make the postseason.

2004 NL WILD CARD

In 2004, the 10th season of the Wild Card, the NL provided another in its seemingly endless run of memorable races. At the All-Star break, 12 of the 16 teams were within five games of a playoff spot. By September a few had dropped off, but eight clubs remained in contention, creating a wonderful mess that captivated fans.

Leading the Wild Card chase were the Giants, basically a one-man team — but that man, Barry Bonds, was enjoying perhaps the greatest season by a hitter. (Bonds won the batting title at .362, and his .609 OBP broke his own record.) Behind the Giants came the Cubs, the Padres, the 2003 world champion Marlins and, trailing all other contenders, the 69-63 Astros.

Houston's hopes appeared slim and its players were surprised that the roster wasn't dismantled at the trade deadline. "They said they weren't going to break up this team because we have great players," reliever Brad Lidge said of Astros management. "With the talent we have, we could have taken off like we did at any time." Take off they did — and then some. With a balanced lineup in which six of eight positions produced at least 20 home runs, the Astros came from eight back of the Giants as late as Aug. 14. "It just shows that you should never give up," first baseman Jeff Bagwell said. "The middle of August was a tough situation. We just kept grinding and grinding and here we are."

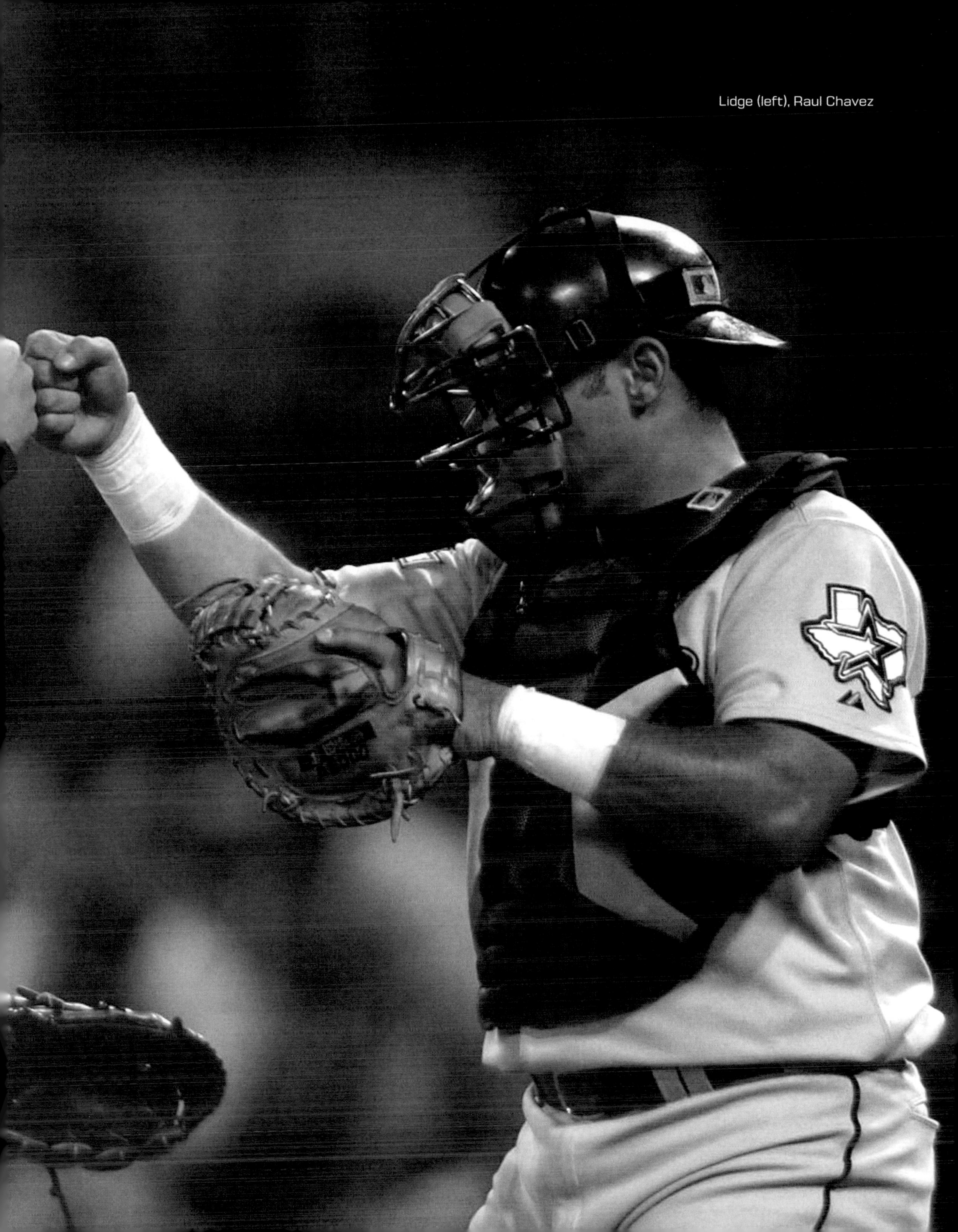

Lidge (left), Raul Chavez

Beltran

CATCHING A STAR

On June 24, 2004, Astros GM Gerry Hunsicker made the biggest gamble of his career. With the Astros virtually out of the pennant race, he traded two players and cash for 27-year-old Royals star Carlos Beltran. Many were shocked that a team that was 37-34, in *fifth* place in the NL Central and tied for sixth in the Wild Card standings, would give up so much to acquire the free agent-to-be. Hunsicker beat other teams to the punch more than a month before the trade deadline, but it seemed a steep price to pay.

Things collapsed almost immediately. By July 30 the Astros trailed by 15.5 games and rumors swirled that Beltran would be traded *again*. But the Astros kept him. On Aug. 22 they had a sub-.500 record and were still sixth in the Wild Card race. On Aug. 27, *Baseball Prospectus* gave Houston a 0.41 percent chance to make the playoffs. But that night, Beltran clubbed two homers in a win.

Houston didn't lose again for two weeks. When that streak ended, they started another one, then another. All told, the Astros

CARLOS BELTRAN'S 2004 POSTSEASON STATS						
	H	R	HR	RBI	SB	AVG
NLDS	10	9	4	9	2	.455
NLCS	10	12	4	5	4	.417

Finley

HOLLYWOOD ENDING

On Oct. 2, the season's second-to-last day, three teams were battling for the final two NL playoff spots. Like a game of musical chairs, just two would make the postseason. The Dodgers, with a two-game lead over the Giants in the NL West, needed to beat San Francisco once to capture the division. The Giants, meanwhile, were tied with Houston for the Wild Card.

With 52 comeback wins already, the Dodgers seemed fated to grab the West. "I don't know if it's magic, but they've got something working for them," Giants reliever Matt Herges told the *Los Angeles Times*. The Giants were about to be victimized by comeback No. 53. Down, 3-0, in the bottom of the ninth, Los Angeles got a single and three walks. Cesar Izturis then hit a certain double-play grounder, but Giants shortstop Cody Ransom — in as a defensive replacement — booted it. The next batter, Jayson Werth, singled to tie the game.

That brought up veteran Steve Finley with the bases loaded, and all Los Angeles needed was a fly ball to win. Finley did one better, launching a shot into the right-field pavilion for the first-ever playoff-clinching, walk-off grand slam. "I wanted it. I knew I was going to get it done," Finley said. "When I walked to the plate, I knew the game was over." The loss dropped San Francisco one game behind Houston, and when both teams won the next day, the Astros emerged with the playoff berth.

finished on a 28-8 tear. On Sept. 26, though, they still trailed the Cubs by 2.5 games and the Giants by two with seven left. From that point on, Chicago went 2-6, San Francisco went 4-3, and Houston won all seven games to capture the Wild Card on the season's final day. Beltran then put up one of the greatest playoff performances ever, making Hunsicker's gamble a smashing success — at least in the short term. "It was more of a high-risk trade than we wanted," he admitted after the season. "We were robbing Peter to pay Paul."

1934 St. Louis Cardinals

1934 NL

The "Gashouse Gang" Cardinals, featuring outsized personalities like brash hurler Dizzy Dean and practical-joking third baseman Pepper Martin, were a famously boisterous club. However, it wasn't all smiles in 1934. "The Cardinals were a combative, rowdy lot, which can be entertaining when a team is winning," wrote Christina Kahrl of *Baseball Prospectus*.

Indeed, behind fiery Manager Frankie Frisch, the unfocused Cards spent most of the season in third place. But in August things suddenly turned around. "The Cards, while undeniably showing themselves as a great fighting team, spent about three-fourths of the year fighting amongst themselves before they finally struck upon the idea of uniting their energies

in a common cause and fighting the enemy," John Drebinger wrote in *The New York Times*.

Coincidentally, that three-quarters mark was about the point at which the front-running Giants began to crack. "As late as Sept. 7," Drebinger wrote, "they held a margin of seven games and, confronted by a home stand with many 'soft touches' dotting the schedule, the task of overhauling them seemed impossible." But the Cardinals deftly performed that task, closing ground in the standings while New York dropped games to weak clubs. After mounting one of history's least likely late-season comebacks, St. Louis moved into a tie for first on Sept. 28. The pennant thus came down to the final two games.

Paul Dean (left),
Dizzy Dean

BROTHERS IN ARMS

Cardinals fans loved Dizzy Dean because he won like nobody else. Reporters loved him because he gave quotes like nobody else. But Cards management both loved and hated Dean — loved him for his talent and exuberance, but hated him for his cockiness and selfishness. ("If there were one more like him in baseball," GM Branch Rickey said, "I'd get out of the game.") In 1934, those conflicting aspects of Dean's persona became the main story of the Cardinals' campaign. First he nearly wrecked the season by walking out on the team, then saved the day upon his return.

The trouble began over money. Dizzy was upset that the Cardinals were paying his younger brother Paul a measly $3,000 yearly salary. Paul was a 21-year-old rookie, but by the end of May he was 5-1, ranking second on the team in wins behind Dizzy. Both brothers repeatedly demanded a raise for Paul, but Rickey refused. Finally, on June 1, the Deans announced that they had sore arms and would be unavailable to pitch until Paul's salary was raised. Rickey stood firm, though, and the contrite brothers returned to the club the next day. The short-lived walkout accomplished nothing except alienating the Deans' teammates.

After the brothers returned, St. Louis went on a 21-21 skid, dropping from first place to third. Things turned uglier in August when Dizzy walked out again, upset because he had been fined for missing an exhibition game. Returning to the team eight days later, he got back in his teammates' good graces the old-fashioned way — by winning. Dizzy went 30-7, the most wins in the league in 17 years, and the Cards eventually grabbed the pennant on a dramatic final weekend during which all three games were won by a Dean.

DIZZY DEAN'S 1934 STATS

IP	W	L	ERA	CG	SHO	K	WHIP
311.2	30	7	2.66	24	7	195	1.165

CAREFUL WHAT YOU WISH FOR

Giants player-manager Bill Terry was cocky, and he had a right to be. In 1933, his first full campaign after taking over as manager, Terry led the Giants to the world championship — and batted .322 for good measure. When he held court with reporters before the next season, though, he let his confidence get the best of him. When asked about the rival Dodgers' chances of winning the pennant, Terry responded with a wise-crack: "Is Brooklyn still in the league?"

It turned out Terry was correct about the Dodgers' prospects; they finished sixth at 71-81. But Terry should have looked at the schedule before poking the Dodgers with a stick. On Sept. 29 his Giants found themselves in a first-place tie with St. Louis. New York's last two games were against, you guessed it, the revenge-minded Dodgers. With thousands of Brooklynites making the cross-town trip to the Polo Grounds specifically to heckle Terry, the inspired Dodgers topped their rivals, 5-1, in the first game and won a 10-inning thriller in the second. When news of the Giants' demise reached the St. Louis clubhouse, the boisterous Cardinals began chanting "Brooklyn's still in the league! Brooklyn's still in the league!" The Cards won the pennant by two games — their largest lead of the season. The Giants, meanwhile, began issuing refunds for all the World Series tickets they had sold.

1914 NL

Nearly a century after it happened, the Boston Braves' comeback — during which they took the NL pennant by rocketing from last place to first in a span of just 37 days — still seems too crazy to believe. In 1950, The Associated Press named the Miracle Braves' run the greatest sports upset of the 20th century. Another 50 years later, there is still no doubt that the Braves remain — with help from the 1969 Mets — the standard by which baseball miracles are measured. They are why the phrase "since 1914" is still a sportswriting staple.

For instance, "Upset Biggest Since 1914," a *New York Times* headline crowed when the Cardinals beat the Yankees in the '42 Series.

The Giants' 1951 surge was "the most tremendous comeback in baseball since 1914," the *Times* proclaimed at the end of that year's famed Dodgers-Giants race.

"The Astros are the first team since the 1914 Braves to make the postseason after being 15 games below .500," *Sports Illustrated* wrote in 2005.

No miracle since has eclipsed what Boston achieved. "The Braves accomplished something no other team has ever accomplished before," the *Times* wrote after Boston finished its season with a World Series sweep of Philadelphia. "It has turned the whole realm of baseball upside down. ... A ball club which started the season as a joke reached the perch deluxe in baseball in a blaze of glory."

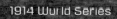
1914 World Series

MIRACLE MAN

Braves Manager George Stallings was a complicated fellow. He was, his biographer Martin Kohout wrote, "a dignified, fastidious Southerner," yet "could fly into a schizophrenic rage at the drop of a pop fly." His nickname was "Gentleman George," yet he once vowed to "knock [Connie] Mack's head off" before a series against the A's.

The 1913 Braves seemed the wrong team for such a short-tempered manager. Boston led the league with 273 errors, and Stallings griped, "I have never seen any club look quite so bad." He soon set about molding the next year's roster to his liking. First he moved promising youngster Hank Gowdy from backup catcher to starter. He stole soon-to-be NL MVP Johnny Evers from the Cubs in a lopsided trade. He showed an unusual amount of confidence in second-year pitchers Bill James and

Dick Rudolph, and was rewarded when they won 26 games apiece.

But the most crucial change Stallings made in 1914 was to institute platooning. With seven journeyman outfielders, but nary a star among them, he hoped to maximize each man's success by batting him only against opposite-handed pitchers. Stallings thus became the first manager to use platooning as a regular strategy. It worked, too. None of the outfielders received 400 at-bats, but three set career highs in average. The outfield carried its weight offensively, allowing the club's strengths — pitching and infield defense — to shine. "This event had tremendous impact on other managers, almost revolutionary impact," wrote historian Bill James (no relation to the pitcher). "From 1915 to 1925, basically all Major League teams platooned at one or more positions."

MOVE OVER, MATTY

On the morning of July 19, Boston woke up in last place. By Aug. 15, when the Braves took the field for the finale of a crucial three-game series against New York, they had vaulted all the way to second, 4.5 games behind the Giants. That afternoon's game was the key contest of the season, for the Braves not only defeated the league's best pitcher, Christy Mathewson, but also completed a sweep that knocked the dazed Giants back on their heels. It was the best-attended game of the year and, *The New York Times* wrote, "one of the most brilliant struggles ever staged at the historic Polo Grounds."

For nine innings, Mathewson and the Braves' diminutive junkballer Lefty Tyler traded shutout frames. The Giants had

a chance to break the 0-0 tie when they loaded the bases in the bottom of the ninth, but Tyler induced a harmless grounder. In the top of the 10th inning, Braves catcher Hank Gowdy — a former Giant whom John McGraw had discarded as not talented enough — ripped an RBI triple. Moments later the flustered Mathewson wild-pitched Gowdy home, making it 2-0 Boston.

The Giants still had a chance in the bottom of the 10th, and they seemed eager to take advantage of it, loading the bases against Tyler with nobody out. But the crafty lefty once again worked his way out of trouble, inducing a pop-up, a strikeout and a feeble grounder. "That last great rally was hurled down to a bitter defeat," the *Times* griped.

James (left),
Stallings (center),
Rudolph

1995 AL WEST

"When I got here, if you wanted to see any people in this place you had to go to a Seahawks game," Mariners ace Randy Johnson said of the Kingdome in 1995. "We're up here in the Northwest, and all we're known for is grunge rock, Starbucks and Microsoft. But now we're becoming a baseball town." Indeed, 1995's AL West race quickly changed Seattle into a baseball-loving city. Like a time-lapse photographic image, a change that ordinarily takes years was compressed into a few weeks. One could feel the difference in the city's vibe virtually overnight.

This was partly because, for the first time, Mariners fans had something to root for. Historically they were the Majors' least accomplished club, having finished with a losing record in 16 of their 18 seasons in existence. Not only had the M's never finished first, but they'd never even finished second. But the '95 team was different. The players were lovable and, more importantly, they were *really good*. Ken Griffey Jr., Edgar Martinez, chrome-domed Jay Buhner and wild-maned Johnson all became Kingdome legends. They weren't dominant — they were 62-61 as late as Sept. 7 in this strike-shortened season — but they were resilient, coming back from 13 games down to force a one-game playoff with the California Angels. "We went from a team that looked like it didn't have a chance to get into the playoffs to playing great in September and all of a sudden getting in," Martinez told ESPN.com's Jonah Keri.

Griffey Jr.

PRODIGAL SON

If you were a baseball fan on May 26, 1995, the image is probably still ingrained in your brain's video archive. Ken Griffey Jr., the exuberant 25-year-old who is the best player in baseball, sprints toward right-center field, glides through the air like Michael Jordan, makes a spectacular backhand catch, and crashes full speed into the padded wall, leaving an imprint from his spikes halfway up the fence. He holds onto the ball, but heartbreakingly, his left wrist is shattered upon impact.

Losing a franchise player of Griffey's caliber would have immediately ended most teams' pennant chances, but the rest of the Mariners picked up the slack as best they could with, among others, a 19-year-old rookie — and future winner of multiple MVP Awards — named Alex Rodriguez. By the time Griffey returned to the diamond on Aug. 15, the Mariners had sunk to third place, 11.5 games out of first. But they weren't out of it quite yet.

STRANGE DAYS

By Sept. 19, the Seattle Mariners had come so close to their goal that they could almost taste it. Trailing California by 11.5 games a mere 25 games earlier, the Mariners were now just two behind. On this night, one of the most dramatic of the season, they were two outs away from losing when light-hitting utility man Doug Strange tied it with just his second home run of the year. In the 11th, a Ken Griffey Jr. walk-off single completed the unlikely win. Five days later came another compelling comeback victory. After coughing up a ninth-inning lead to Oakland, the Mariners entered the bottom of the ninth trailing against Hall of Fame closer Dennis Eckersley. But Edgar Martinez singled and Tino Martinez (no relation) hit a walk-off home run that sent the Kingdome into bedlam. The M's now led the AL West by two games, and the race was theirs to lose.

TWO OF A KIND

For Angels veteran Mark Langston, starting the one-game playoff essentially meant overcoming a young version of himself: Randy Johnson. Both were powerful lefties who once struggled with control. Both won strikeout crowns with the Mariners. After harnessing their control, they now ranked 1-2 on Seattle's all-time wins list. They were even traded for each other in 1989. In '95, Langston was near the end of his career while Johnson, with an 18-2 record, had established himself as the AL's best pitcher.

Langston started the game in strong fashion, shutting out the M's until the fifth, but he was no match for Johnson, who carried a no-hitter into the sixth. Langston fell apart in the seventh, giving up four runs in part to his own error. It got worse from there, as Langston got into a heated argument with teammate Rex Hudler in the dugout while the Mariners' lead stretched to 9-0.

With the outcome no longer in doubt, Johnson gave up a solo homer in the ninth, but then struck out Tim Salmon — his 12th K — to complete the 9-1 victory. "We rode, like we have all year, on Randy's big shoulders," M's Manager Lou Piniella told the *Seattle Times*. "This was his game. No one was going to take it away from him."

Langston

SOURCE NOTES

INTRO

6-7. Enders, Eric. "Armando Marsans." Published in Tom Simon, editor, *Deadball Stars of the National League*. Washington, DC: Brassey's, 2004.

6-7. Saroyan, William. "My Baseball." *Sports Illustrated*, Oct. 8, 1956.

6-7. Gould, Stephen Jay. *Triumph and Tragedy in Mudville: A Lifelong Passion for Baseball*. New York: W.W. Norton, 2004.

CHAPTER 1

8-13. Anderson, Dave. "Pitcher's Lib Movement?" *The New York Times*, Nov. 8, 1978.

8-13. Chass, Murray. "Martin Resigns; Bob Lemon to Manage Yankees." *The New York Times*, July 25, 1978.

8-13. Chass, Murray. "Martin Will Rejoin Yanks As Club's Manager in 1980." *The New York Times*, July 30, 1978.

8-13. Chass, Murray. "Owner Stunned By Manager's Outburst." *The New York Times*, July 24, 1978.

8-13. "Dent homer puts an end to Sox saga." Uncredited United Press International article published in the *Newport Daily News*, Oct. 3, 1978.

8-13. Eskenazi, Gerald. "Rice is M.V.P., Guidry 2d." *The New York Times*, Nov. 8, 1978.

8-13. May, Peter. "Reggie has kind words for Red Sox." United Press International article published in the *Newport Daily News*, Oct. 3, 1978.

8-13. May, Peter. "The Boston Massacre…" United Press International article published in the *Newport Daily News*, Sept. 11, 1978.

8-13. Richman, Milt. "Steinbrenner Praises Dent." United Press International article published in the *Newport Daily News*, Oct. 3, 1978.

8-13. Richman, Milt. "Yastrzemski Stung By Defeat." United Press International article published in the *Newport Daily News*, Oct. 3, 1978.

8-13. Rogers, Thomas. "Reporter's Notebook: Yank Bickering Revives." *The New York Times*, May 20, 1978.

14-21. Alou, Felipe. Interview with the author, 2001.

14-21. Davis, Tommy. Interview with the author, Aug. 2002.

14-21. Einstein, Charles. *Willie's Time: Baseball's Golden Age*. Carbondale, IL: Southern Illinois University Press, 2004.

14-21. "Mays Faints in Dugout." Associated Press article published in *The New York Times*, Sept. 13, 1962.

14-21. Neyer, Rob. *Rob Neyer's Big Book of Baseball Blunders*. New York: Fireside, 2006.

14-21. Roseboro, John, with Bill Libby. *Glory Days With the Dodgers and Other Days With Others*. New York: Atheneum, 1978.

14-21. "Speed Makes the Dodgers Go." *Life*, Sept. 28, 1962, p. 49.

14-21. Stout, Glenn, and Richard A. Johnson. *The Dodgers: 120 Years of Dodgers Baseball*. New York: Houghton Mifflin, 2004.

14-21. Travers, Steven. *A Tale of Three Cities: The 1962 Baseball Season in New York, Los Angeles, and San Francisco*. Dulles, VA: Potomac Books, 2009.

14-21. Wills, Maury. Interview with the author, Aug. 2002.

22-23. "The Baseball Season." *The New York Times*, Oct. 12, 1904.

22-23. McElreavy, Wayne. "Jack Chesbro." Published in Jones, David, editor, *Deadball Stars of the American League*. Dulles, VA: Potomac Books, 2006.

24-25. Charlton, James. *The Baseball Chronology: The Complete History of the Most Important Events in the Game of Baseball*. New York: Macmillan, 1991.

24-25. Felber, Bill. *A Game of Brawl: The Orioles, the Beaneaters, and the Battle for the 1897 Pennant*. Lincoln: University of Nebraska Press, 2007.

24-25. Solomon, Burt. *Where They Ain't: The Fabled Life and Untimely Death of the Original Baltimore Orioles, the Team That Gave Birth to Modern Baseball*. New York: The Free Press, 1999.

24-25. "The Orioles Fall." *The Washington Morning Times*, Sept. 28, 1897, p. 6.

26-31. Armour, Mark. "Vern Stephens." The Baseball Biography Project, published by the Society for American Baseball Research at bioproj.sabr.org; accessed Oct. 29, 2009.

26-31. Cramer, Richard Ben. *DiMaggio: The Hero's Life*. New York: Simon & Schuster, 2001.

26-31. Drebinger, John. "Parnell Racks Up 25th Triumph, 4-1." *The New York Times*, Sept. 26, 1949.

26-31. Drebinger, John. "Red Sox Score, 3-0." *The New York Times*, Sept. 25, 1949.

26-31. Drebinger, John. "Yankees Lose Lead for First Time; 66,156 See Red Sox Win in 8th, 7-6." *The New York Times*, Sept. 27, 1949.

26-31. Drebinger, John. "Yanks Whip Red Sox in Season Finale To Win 16th American League Pennant." *The New York Times*, Oct. 3, 1949.

26-31. Effrat, Louis. "Mapes and Grieve Near Fisticuffs on Squeeze Play After Yankees' Setback." *The New York Times*, Sept. 27, 1949.

26-31. Goldman, Steven, editor. *It Ain't Over 'Til It's Over: The Baseball Prospectus Pennant Race Book*. New York: Basic Books, 2007.

26-31. Halberstam, David. *Summer of '49*. New York: Harper Perennial, 2002.

26-31. Halberstam, David. *The Teammates: A Portrait of a Friendship*. New York: Hyperion, 2004.

26-31. "Kell Batting Victor; Indians Get 3d Place." Associated Press article published in *The New York Times*, Oct. 3, 1949.

26-31. Smith, Red. "Beginning of the End?" *The New York Times*, Sept. 27, 1949.

CHAPTER 2

32-37. Honig, Donald. *A Donald Honig Reader*. New York: Fireside, 1988.

32-37. James, Bill, and Rob Neyer. *The Neyer/James Guide to Pitchers*. New York: Fireside, 1988.

32-37. Peary, Danny, editor. *We Played the Game: 65 Players Remember Baseball's Greatest Era, 1947-1964*. New York: Hyperion, 1994.

32-37. Snider, Duke, with Bill Gilbert. *The Duke of Flatbush*. New York: Zebra Books, 1988.

32-37. Stout, Glenn, and Richard A. Johnson. *The Dodgers: 120 Years of Dodgers Baseball*. New York: Houghton Mifflin, 2004.

38-39. Atkins, Harry. "Alexander blanks Red Sox for Tigers." Associated Press article published in the *Journal Tribune* (Biddeford, ME), Sept. 15, 1987.

38-39. Boswell, Thomas. "Baseball's Hired Gun Could Care Less About the Race." Washington Post Syndicate article published in the *Syracuse Post-Standard*, Sept. 28, 1987.

38-39. McClary, Mike. "October Surprise Part 8 — Tigers Pull Ahead." Published at dailyfungo.com, Oct. 3, 2009; accessed Oct. 30, 2009.

40-41. Giglio, James N. *Musial: From Stash to Stan the Man*. Columbia, MO: University of Missouri Press, 2007.

42-45. "2008 Turkeys Of The Year: The Mets' Bullpen." Published at sportsillustrated.cnn.com, Nov. 25, 2008; accessed Oct. 30, 2009.

42-45. Hubbuch, Bart. "Hamels Can't Stop Dissing Mets." *New York Post*, Feb. 24, 2009.

42-45. Jaffe, Jay. "Prospectus Hit and Run: The Mets Bullpen Failures." Published at, baseballprospectus.com, Sept. 25, 2008; accessed Oct. 30, 2008.

42-45. Marchman, Tim. "Mets Bullpen a Cause For Concern." *New York Sun*, Feb. 29, 2008.

42-45. Zolecki, Todd. "Is it 2007 Again?" Published at philly.com, Aug. 27, 2008; accessed Oct. 30, 2008.

46-47. Fimrite, Ron. "L.A. Was Snuffed Out At Candlestick." *Sports Illustrated*, Oct. 11, 1982.

46-47. Schulman, Henry. "Candlestick Classics #3: Day of Sweet Revenge." *San Francisco Chronicle*, Sept. 7, 1999.

46-47. "Sports People; Mascot Won't Return." *The New York Times*, Jan. 19, 1986.

46-47. Weisman, Jon. *100 Things Dodgers Fans Should Know & Do Before They Die*. Chicago: Triumph Books, 2009.

48-53. "Indians Conquer Athletics Twice Before 82,781, New Major Record." *The New York Times*, June 21, 1948.

48-53. "Indians Top Athletics 5-3, 2-0, Move Within Half Game of First." *The New York Times*, Sept. 20, 1948.

48-53. Daley, Arthur. "Still Feudin', Fussin' and Fightin'." *The New York Times*, Oct. 3, 1948.

48-53. Dawson, James P. "Wild Celebration by Winning Team." *The New York Times*, Oct. 5, 1948.

48-53. Goldman, Steven, editor. *It Ain't Over 'Til It's Over: The Baseball Prospectus Pennant Race Book*. New York: Basic Books, 2007.

48-53. Veeck, Bill, with Ed Linn. *Veeck — As in Wreck*. Chicago: University of Chicago Press, 2001.

54-59. Clark, Brooks. "A Roundup Of The Week Jan. 28-Feb. 3." *Sports Illustrated*, Feb. 11, 1980.

54-59. Duncan, Chris. "Joe Niekro Remembered for Sense of Humor." Associated Press article published at foxnews.com, Oct. 28, 2006; accessed Nov. 3, 2009.

54-59. Hollander, Dave. J.R. "Richard: The Human Condition." *Houston Press*, Sept. 2, 2004.

54-59. Jarrin, Jaime. Interview with the author, April 29, 2008.

54-59. Nack, William. "Now Everyone Believes Him." *Sports Illustrated*, Aug.18, 1980.

54-59. Pearlman, Jeff. "Astros are forgetting one of their legends." Published at ESPN.com, April 4, 2007; accessed Nov. 3, 2009.

54-59. "Player Moves." *Winnipeg Free Press*, Sept. 9, 1980, p. 101.

54-59. Stout, Glenn, and Richard A. Johnson. *The Dodgers: 120 Years of Dodgers Baseball*. New York: Houghton Mifflin, 2004.

54-59. Weintraub, Robert. "The Last Real Race." Published at ESPN.com, Sept. 26, 2007; accessed Nov. 3, 2009.

54-59. Weisman, Jon. *100 Things Dodgers Fans Should Know & Do Before They Die*. Chicago: Triumph Books, 2009.

54-59. Wilker, Josh. "J.R. Richard, 1979." Published at cardboardgods.net, Jan. 26, 2007; accessed Nov. 3, 2009.

60-63. Verducci, Tom. "Double Trouble." *Sports Illustrated*, Sept. 6, 1993.

60-63. Weintraub, Robert. "The Last Real Race." Published at ESPN.com, Sept. 26, 2007; accessed Nov. 3, 2009.

CHAPTER 3

64-67. Goldman, Steven, editor. *It Ain't Over 'Til It's Over: The Baseball Prospectus Pennant Race Book*. New York: Basic Books, 2007.

64-67. Heidenry, John, and Brett Topel. *The Boys Who Were Left Behind: The 1944 World Series between the Hapless St. Louis Browns and the Legendary St. Louis Cardinals*. Lincoln, NE: University of Nebraska Press, 2006.

64-67. Mead, William B. *Even the Browns*. Chicago: Contemporary Books, 1978.

68-69. Campbell, Dave. "Twins complete comeback, 6-5 over Tigers in 12th." Associated Press article published at yahoo.com, Oct. 6, 2009; accessed Nov. 5, 2009.

68-69. "Ordonez comes through in clutch, again, as Tigers grow Central lead." Associated Press article published at ESPN.com, Sept. 30, 2009; accessed Nov. 5, 2009.

68-69. Silver, Nate. "The Greatest Pennant Race Comebacks." Published at baseballprospectus.com, Oct. 4, 2007; accessed Nov. 5, 2009.

68-69. "Twins Playoff Odds Day By Day." Published at baseballprospectus.com, Oct. 20, 2009; accessed Nov. 5, 2009.

70-75. Creamer, Robert. "The Transistor Kid." *Sports Illustrated*, May 4, 1964.

70-75. Goldman, Steven, editor. *It Ain't Over 'Til It's Over: The Baseball Prospectus Pennant Race Book*. New York: Basic Books, 2007.

70-75. Peary, Danny, editor. *We Played the Game: 65 Players Remember Baseball's Greatest Era, 1947-1964*. New York: Hyperion, 1994.

70-75. Terrell, Roy. "At Last the Twain Do Meet." *Sports Illustrated*, April 14, 1958.

70-75. Terrell, Roy. "They Call It Baseball." *Sports Illustrated*, April 13, 1959.

CHAPTER 4

76-83. Friend, Tom. "From San Diego's favorite son ... to spoilsport." *ESPN The Magazine*, Feb. 13, 2008.

76-83. Gilbert, Steve, Jason Gray, and David Briggs. "Notes: Hershiser gives Webb support." MLB.com article published Aug. 21, 2007; accessed Nov. 5, 2009.

76-83. Kahrl, Christina. "Oops, They Did it Again?" Published at baseballprospectus.com, Oct. 4, 2009; accessed Nov. 6, 2009.

76-83. Kiszla, Mark. "Touching display, or not." *The Denver Post*, Oct. 2, 2007.

76-83. Krasovic, Tom. "Hoffman took it hard." *U-T Sportsblog*, published by San Diego Union-Tribune, signonsandiego.com, Oct. 1, 2007.

76-83. Marchman, Tim. "The Mystical Collapse of a Bullpen." *The New York Sun*, Sept. 28, 2007.

76-83. "Ramirez's big day leads surging Cubs to another win." Associated Press article published at ESPN.com, July 20, 2007; accessed Nov. 5, 2009.

76-83. "Rollins, Phillies confident about chances in '07." Associated Press article published at ESPN.com, January 23, 2007; accessed Nov. 5, 2009.

76-83. Saunders, Patrick. "Rox Roll: 21 victories in 22 games." *The Denver Post*, Oct. 16, 2007.

76-83. Silver, Nate. "The Greatest Pennant Race Comebacks." Published at baseballprospectus.com, Oct. 4, 2007; accessed Nov. 5, 2009.

76-83. Singer, Tom. "Coins flipped for tie-breaker scenarios." MLB.com article published Sept. 7, 2007; accessed Nov.5, 2009.

76-83. "Streak over, Webb now eyes 2nd Cy Young." Associated Press article published at nbcsports.msnbc.com, Aug. 23, 2007; accessed Nov. 5, 2009.

84-87. Leggett, William. "A Wild Finale — and It's Boston!" *Sports Illustrated*, Oct. 9, 1967.

84-87. Mulvoy, Mark. "Now Playing in Right Field…" *Sports Illustrated*, April 7, 1969.

84-87. Mulvoy, Mark. "Virtue is Rewarded." *Sports Illustrated*, Aug. 21, 1967.

84-87. "Sportsman Of The Year." *Sports Illustrated*, Dec. 25, 1967.

88-89. Smiles, Jack. *Big Ed Walsh: The Life and Times of a Spitballing Hall of Famer*. Jefferson, NC: McFarland, 2007.

88-89. Turner, Jamie. "Perfect flashback: On Oct. 2, 1908, Joss gem triumphs in Cleveland's greatest pitching duel." *Cleveland Plain Dealer*, Oct. 1, 2008; accessed Nov. 6, 2009.

90-93. Jordan, Pat. "Pitcher in Search of a Pitch." *Sports Illustrated*, April 15, 1974.

90-93. Leggett, William. "Churned By the Gut-grinder." *Sports Illustrated*, Sept. 24, 1973.

90-93. "Next Week." *Sports Illustrated*, Sept. 17, 1973.

90-93. Goldman, Steven, editor. *It Ain't Over 'Til It's Over: The Baseball Prospectus Pennant Race Book*. New York: Basic Books, 2007.

90-93. Markusen, Bruce. *Roberto Clemente: The Great One*. Champaign, IL: Sports Publishing, 1998.

94-97. Enders, Eric. "Armando Marsans." Published in Tom Simon, editor, *Deadball Stars of the National League*. Washington, DC: Brassey's, 2004.

94-97. "Federal League: Chicago Splits Double-Header and Leads Pittsburgh." *The New York Times*, Oct. 4, 1915.

94-97. Koppett, Leonard. *Koppett's Concise History of Major League Baseball*. New York: Carroll & Graf, 2004.

94-97. Macht, Norman Lee. *Connie Mack and the Early Years of Baseball*. Lincoln, NE: University of Nebraska Press, 2007.

94-97. Thorn, John, and Pete Palmer, editors. *Total Baseball*. New York: Warner Books, 1989.

98-101. Creamer, Robert, and Roy Terrell. "The Great Drama: Last Act." *Sports Illustrated*, Oct. 8, 1956.

98-101. Peary, Danny, editor. *We Played the Game: 65 Players Remember Baseball's Greatest Era, 1947-1964*. New York: Hyperion, 1994.

98-101. Saroyan, William. "My Baseball." *Sports Illustrated*, Oct. 8, 1956.

98-101. Stout, Glenn, and Richard A. Johnson. *The Dodgers: 120 Years of Dodgers Baseball*. New York: Houghton Mifflin, 2004.

102-03. Goldman, Steven, editor. *It Ain't Over 'Til It's Over: The Baseball Prospectus Pennant Race Book*. New York: Basic Books, 2007.

104-07. Amman, Larry, and L. Robert Davids. "Baseball Brothers." Published in *Baseball Research Journal*. Cooperstown, NY: SABR, 1979.

104-07. Carry, Peter. "Baseball's Week." *Sports Illustrated*, Sept. 22, 1969.

104-07. Carry, Peter. "Highlight." *Sports Illustrated*, Sept.22, 1969.

104-07. Carry, Peter. "Mad Scramble East And West…." *Sports Illustrated*, Sept. 22, 1969.

104-07. "Pitching — and An Omen — favors The Mets." *Sports Illustrated*, Oct. 6, 1969.

104-07. Weiskopf, Herman. "Baseball's Week." *Sports Illustrated*, Sept. 8, 1969.

CHAPTER 5

108-113. Enders, Eric. "Stranger Than Fiction." *2008 Official NLCS Program*. New York: MLB Properties, 2008.

108-113. Goldman, Steven, editor. *It Ain't Over 'Til It's Over: The Baseball Prospectus Pennant Race Book*. New York: Basic Books, 2007.

108-113. Murphy, Cate. *Crazy '08: How a Cast of Cranks, Rogues, Boneheads, and Magnates Created the Greatest Year in Baseball History*. New York: Harper Paperbacks, 2008.

108-113. Ritter, Lawrence S. *The Glory of Their Times*. New York: William Morrow, 1984.

114-17. Eskenazi, Gerald. "Marichal Suspended 8 Playing Dates, Fined $1,750; Dodgers Beat Mets, 8-4." *The New York Times*, Aug. 24, 1965.

114-17. Mann, Jack. "Deadly Slide For The Dodgers." *Sports Illustrated*, May 10, 1965.

114-17. Roseboro, John, with Bill Libby. *Glory Days With the Dodgers and Other Days With Others*. New York: Atheneum, 1978.

114-17. "They Said It." *Sports Illustrated*, Oct. 11, 1965.

118-23. Phelon, W.A. "How the New World's Championship was Won." *Baseball Magazine*, Dec. 1920.

118-23. "Comment on Current Events in Sports." *The New York Times*, Sept. 13, 1920.

118-23. Coughlin, Dan. "1920 — a Year of Tragedy and Triumph for the Indians." *The Sporting News*, Oct. 24, 1970.

118-23. Enders, Eric. *The Fall Classic: The Definitive History of the World Series*. New York: Sterling, 2007.

118-23. Jensen, Don. "Ray Chapman." Published in Jones, David, editor, *Deadball Stars of the American League*. Dulles, VA: Potomac Books, 2006.

118-23. Mails, Walter "Duster." "The Pitcher Who Cinched Cleveland's First Pennant." *Baseball Magazine*, Dec. 1920.

118-23. Sandoval, Jim. "Eddie Cicotte." Published in Jones, David, editor, *Deadball Stars of the American League*. Dulles, VA: Potomac Books, 2006.

118-23. "White Sox Drop Behind." *The New York Times*, Oct. 2, 1920.

118-23. Wood, Allan. "Babe Ruth." Published in Jones, David, editor, *Deadball Stars of the American League*. Dulles, VA: Potomac Books, 2006.

118-23. Wood, Allan. "Carl Mays." Published in Jones, David, editor, *Deadball Stars of the American League*. Dulles, VA: Potomac Books, 2006.

124-27. Carry, Peter. "Player of the Week." *Sports Illustrated*, Sept. 21, 1964.

124-27. "Cubs Get Broglio in Trade With Cardinals." UPI article published in *The New York Times*, June 16, 1964.

124-27. Leggett, William. "Futile Surge Amid The Shuffle." *Sports Illustrated*, Sept. 21, 1964.

124-27. Neyer, Rob. *Rob Neyer's Big Book of Baseball Blunders*. New York: Fireside, 2006.

124-27. Peary, Danny, editor. *We Played the Game: 65 Players Remember Baseball's Greatest Era, 1947-1964*. New York: Hyperion, 1994.

CHAPTER 6

128-35. Anderson, Dave. "Sports of The Times; Branca Knew '51 Giants Stole Signs." *The New York Times*, Feb. 1, 2001.

128-35. Canan, Michael. "50 years later Shot still echoing." Scripps Howard News Service article published in *The Post* (Athens, OH), Oct. 3, 2001.

128-35. Enders, Eric. "Big-Time D." *2009 Official World Series Program*. New York: MLB Properties, 2009.

128-35. Heyman, John. "Shot in the Heart: Branca Finally Free to Speak Truth About '51 Home Run." Published at sportsillustrated.cnn.com, Oct. 3, 2006; accessed Nov. 29, 2009.

128-35. Kurkjian, Tim. "What's in store for the victim of No. 756? Ask these guys." *ESPN The Magazine*, July 20, 2007.

128-35. McGowen, Roscoe. "Brooks Beat Phils in Fourteenth, 9-8." *The New York Times*, Oct. 1, 1951.

128-35. Miller, Stuart. *The 100 Greatest Days in New York Sports*. New York: Houghton Mifflin Harcourt, 2006.

128-35. Prager, Joshua. *The Echoing Green: The Untold Story of Bobby Thomson, Ralph Branca and the Shot Heard Round the World*. New York: Random House, 2008.

128-35. Schweppe, Robert. "Don Newcombe Q&A." Published at walteromalley.com, undated; accessed Nov. 29, 2009.

128-35. Smith, Red. *Red Smith on Baseball: The Game's Greatest Writer on the Game's Greatest Years*. Chicago: Ivan R. Dee, 2000.

136-39. Eisenbath, Mike. *Cardinals Encyclopedia*. Philadelphia: Temple University Press, 1999.

136-39. Honig, Donald. *A Donald Honig Reader*. New York: Fireside, 1988.

136-39. McGowen, Roscoe. "Cards Down Brooklyn, 8-5 and 7-6, Homer in 11th Deciding Nightcap." *The New York Times*, July 20, 1942.

136-39. "Major League Averages." *The New York Times*, July 19, 1942.

140-43. "Dodgers in playoffs for first time since '96." Associated Press article published at ESPN.com, Oct. 2, 2004; accessed Nov. 30, 2009.

140-43. Reid, Jason. "Reveling in Their Moments." *Los Angeles Times*, Oct. 3, 2004.

140-43. Schulman, Henry. "Astros GM had doubts on trade." *San Francisco Chronicle*, Oct. 20, 2004.

140-43. Silver, Nate. "The Greatest Pennant Race Comebacks." Published at baseballprospectus.com, Oct. 4, 2007; accessed Nov. 30, 2009.

144-47. "Cards Celebrate Pennant Victory." *The New York Times*, Oct. 1, 1934.

144-47. Drebinger, John. "Cards Rout Reds and Win Pennant As Giants Are Beaten by Dodgers." *The New York Times*, Oct. 1, 1934.

144-47. Drebinger, John. "Past Series Stars in Cast of Cards." *The New York Times*, Oct. 1, 1934.

144-47. "Flatbush Fans Are Gleeful as Dodgers Prove They Are Still in the League." *The New York Times*, Sept. 30, 1934.

144-47. "Giants to Start Refund." *The New York Times*, Oct. 1, 1934.

144-47. Goldman, Steven, editor. *It Ain't Over 'Til It's Over: The Baseball Prospectus Pennant Race Book*. New York: Basic Books, 2007.

148-151. "Baseball At Its Best." *The New York Times*, Oct. 1, 1951.

148-151. "'Big Six' Falls Before Braves." *The New York Times*, Aug. 16, 1914.

148-151. "Braves Capture World's Series in Four Straight." *The New York Times*, Oct. 14, 1914.

148-151. Drebinger, John. "Cards Down Yanks With Homer By 4-2; Win World Series." *The New York Times*, Oct. 6, 1942.

148-151. Enders, Eric. *The Fall Classic: The Definitive History of the World Series*. New York: Sterling, 2007.

148-151. James, Bill. *The Bill James Guide to Baseball Managers From 1870 to Today*. New York: Scribner, 1997.

148-151. Jones, David. "Bill James." Published in Tom Simon, editor, *Deadball Stars of the National League*. Washington, DC: Brassey's, 2004.

148-151. Kohout, Martin. "George Stallings." Published in Tom Simon, editor, *Deadball Stars of the National League*. Washington, DC: Brassey's, 2004.

152-55. DiGiovanna, Mike, and John Weyler. "Langston, Hudler Have Brief, Angry Exchange During the Heat of Playoff Battle." *Los Angeles Times*, Oct. 3, 1995.

152-55. Finnigan, Bob. "Emotional Playoff Win For AL West Title Melts Away Franchise's Years Of Frustration." *Seattle Times*, Oct. 3, 1995.

152-55. "Fracture to Cost Griffey 3 Months." *The New York Times*, May 28, 1995.

152-55. Keri, Jonah. "1995 Mariners: Ringless in Seattle." Published at ESPN.com, April 4, 2008; accessed Nov. 30, 2009.

CREDITS

INDEX

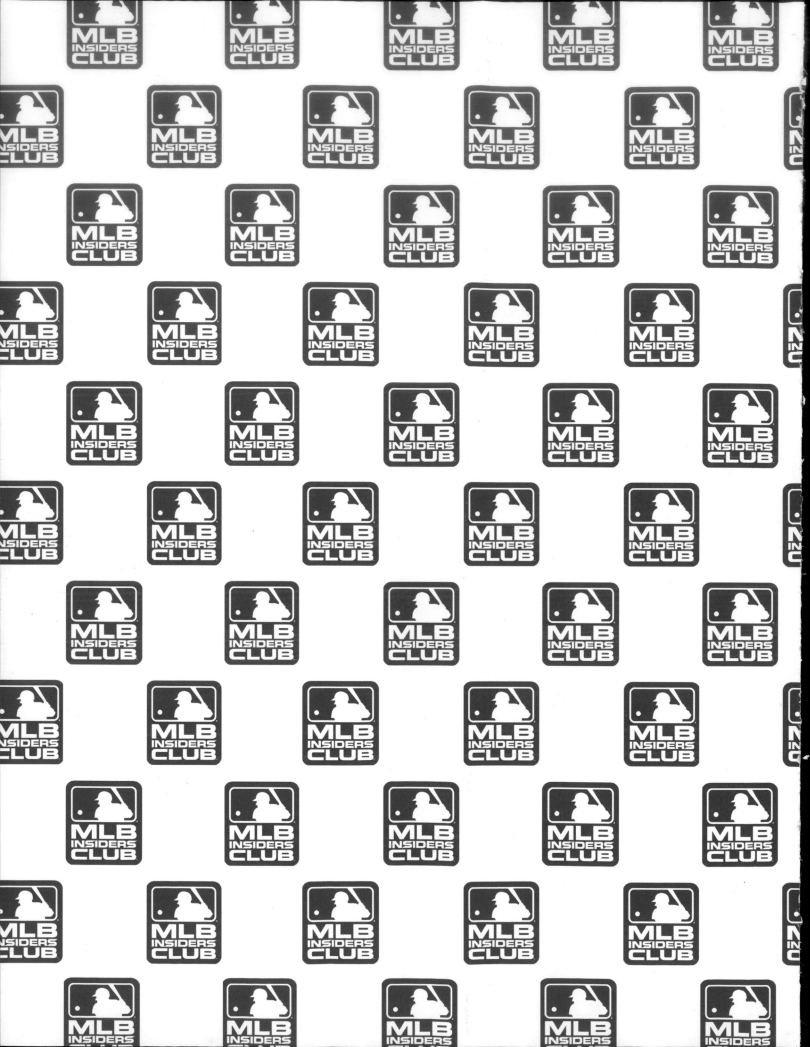